SELF-DEFENSE
FOR PEACEABLE PEOPLE

SELF-DEFENSE
FOR PEACEABLE
PEOPLE

Master J.G. Townsend

with the staff and students of
The Tao-Zen Academy
of Traditional Martial Arts

BLUE SNAKE BOOKS

Berkeley, California

Published by Blue Snake Books

Blue Snake Books
are distributed by North Atlantic Books   Cover photograph by John G. Townsend
P.O. Box 12327   Cover and text design by Brad Greene
Berkeley, California 94712   Printed in the United States of America

Self-Defense for Peaceable People is sponsored by the Society for the Study of Native Arts and Sciences,
a nonprofit educational corporation whose goals are to develop an educational and cross-cultural
perspective linking various scientific, social, and artistic fields; to nurture a holistic view of arts, sciences, humanities, and healing; and to publish and distribute literature on the relationship of mind,
body, and nature.

Blue Snake Books' publications are available through most bookstores. For further
information, call 800-733-3000 or visit our websites at www.northatlanticbooks.com
or www.bluesnakebooks.com.

PLEASE NOTE: The creators and publishers of this book disclaim any liabilities for loss in connection with following any of the practices, exercises, and advice contained herein. To reduce the chance
of injury or any other harm, the reader should consult a professional before undertaking this or any
other martial arts, movement, meditative arts, health, or exercise program. The instructions and
advice printed in this book are not in any way intended as a substitute for legitimate training in an
authentic school of traditional martial art under qualified instruction, or for medical, mental, or emotional counseling with a licensed physician or healthcare provider.

Library of Congress Cataloging-in-Publication Data

Townsend, J. G. (John G.), 1945–
    Self-defense for peaceable people / by Master J.G. Townsend ; with the staff
    and students of The Tao-Zen Academy of Traditional Martial Arts.
        p. cm.
    Summary: "J.G. Townsend teaches the techniques, tactics, and underlying
principles of basic self-defense, so that anyone can learn, at their own pace, how
to apply the power of that knowledge effectively in real-world situations, regardless of size, gender, age, or strength"—Provided by publisher.
    Includes bibliographical references.
    ISBN-13: 978-1-58394-156-0 (trade paper)
    ISBN-10: 1-58394-156-8 (trade paper)
1. Self-defense. I. Title.
    GV1111.T69 2006
    613.6'6—dc22
                                                              2006010176
                                                                     CIP

        2 3 4 5 6 7 8 9 DATA 14 13 12 11 10 09 08

DEDICATION

To my teachers, who went before,
and taught me how to be a better student;
and to my students, who come after,
and show me how to be a better teacher.

—Master J.G. Townsend
Pioneer Hill Dojang
Summer 2005

FOR THE TRUE MARTIAL ARTIST, the best defense is to avoid conflict whenever possible. In this book, you will learn a number of tools for self-defense that you use at your own risk, and it is your responsibility to use no more force than is necessary to defend yourself. Use these tools wisely, compassionately, and in a manner appropriate to the circumstances.

TABLE OF CONTENTS

Foreword . . . XI

How to Use This Book . . . XIV

I. THEORY . . . 1

The Taoist Perspective in Traditional Martial Arts . . . 3

Evening the Odds . . . 4

Introduction to the Shindo Theory of Kinetics . . . 5

    Force and Power . . . 9

    Your Personal Space: Maai and the Sphere of Influence . . . 10

    T'an T'ien, Breathing, and Ch'i . . . 12

    Centerline . . . 15

    Line of Attack . . . 16

    Breaking the Root . . . 17

Awareness and Avoidance . . . 18

Evasion: When Avoidance Fails . . . 19

Improving Your People-Reading Skills . . . 20

Open-Hand Techniques . . . 22

Situationally Appropriate Response . . . 23

Perseverance . . . 24

II. TECHNIQUES . . . 27

Techniques: The Tools of the Trade . . . 29

Building Your Self-Defense Toolbox . . . 30

Setting Up . . . 31

Kihap: The Power Shout . . . 34

Whole-Body Power . . . 35

Stances . . . 39

Basic Blocks . . . 43

   Low Block . . . 45

   Middle Block . . . 45

   High Block . . . 46

   Crossing Hammer Block . . . 46

Crescent Steps . . . 47

Carry the Water . . . 49

Natural Weapons: The Tools You Were Born With . . . 51

Warrior Talk . . . 53

Palm Heel . . . 55

Shuto—The Sword Hand . . . 57

Side Fist Hammer / Forefist . . . 59

Biu Ji—Shooting Fingers . . . 61

Eagle Wing . . . 65

Empi—Elbow Weapons . . . 67

Kicks . . . 69

   Front ("Snap") Kick . . . 69

   Side Kick . . . 71

   Back Kick . . . 71

   Cobra Kick . . . 72

Moo-Rop: Knee Weapons . . . 75

The Infamous Head Butt . . . 77

Drops: Throws, Sweeps, and Take-downs . . . 81

    Forward/Front Drop . . . 82

    Rear Drop . . . 83

III. APPLICATIONS . . . 85

Applications: Defensive Responses . . . 87

Strikes . . . 91

    Strike Defense #1: Close-Range Body Punch . . . 92

    Head Punch Defense #1 . . . 94

    Punch Defense #1 . . . 96

Grabs and Captures . . . 99

    Rear Arm Grab Defense #1 . . . 100

    Rear Arm Grab Defense #2 . . . 102

    Breast Grope / Shoulder "Hug" . . . 103

    Two Assailants—Arm Grab . . . 104

    Front Hair Grab Defense #1 . . . 106

    Rear Hair Grab Defense #1 . . . 108

    Lapel Grab Defense #1 . . . 110

    Front Wrist Grab . . . 112

    Front Shoulder Grab . . . 114

    Headlock Defense #1 . . . 116

Chokes and Strangleholds . . . 119

    Standing Front Choke #1 . . . 120

    Standing Front Choke #2 . . . 122

    Standing Rear Choke Defense #1 . . . 124

    Standing Rear Choke Defense #2 . . . 126

    Rear Arm Bar Choke Defense #1 . . . 127

Groundwork . . . 131

   Groundwork Defense #1: Straddle Strangle, Both Arms Free . . . 131

Weapon Defenses . . . 135

   Stick/Club Defense #1 . . . 136

   Knife Defense #1 . . . 138

IV. APPENDICES . . . 141

A Very Brief History of Unarmed Self-Defense . . . 143

   The Ancestral Arts . . . 143

   Tao-Zen Ryu Shindo . . . 145

Finding the Right School for You . . . 145

Outfitting Your Own Gym—Affordably . . . 148

Bibliography . . . 153

Acknowledgments . . . 155

About the Author . . . 159

FOREWORD

With this book, my purpose is to provide readers with a working understanding of the fundamental theories, tactics, and techniques of basic
self-defense, and their practical application in real-world defensive situations.

I sincerely hope that you never need all of this information, and in a
perfect world, such knowledge would be unnecessary. Respect would be
the order of the day, and we could all go our way in peace. For most of
us, in fact, that's the way it is—most of the time.

Unhappily, however, the world is not perfect, and there is a very real
possibility that a time may come when you might need this knowledge.
I'm not interested in raising alarms with statistics about how often vio-
lence does occur each minute and hour of every day—it happens. None
of us can guarantee that we will never be the targets of aggression. We *can*
refuse to be easy victims. The point is that if such a time ever does come,
you can be confident and prepared to deal with it *effectively*. This book
shows you how.

The techniques presented here are drawn from the Tao-Zen Ryu Shindo
system of martial arts, and they are specifically designed to work effectively for all practitioners, regardless of size or strength. Of course, it is not
possible to demonstrate all of the intricacies of this form in these pages,
but this book offers the fundamentals of practical self-defense. If you
would like to know more about this martial art form, see the Appendix.

When illustrating how the tools and tactics of effective self-defense can
work for defenders regardless of size or strength, I sometimes invoke the

analogy of a bullfight, in which the *toreador* usually evades the larger and stronger bull by fighting smarter, rather than harder—precisely the "secret" of the techniques taught here.

One of my lead students, for example, is a young woman who weighs less than 100 pounds. At one of her early belt tests some years ago, her mother watched in open-mouthed amazement as her daughter threw a fellow student across the room—a shipyard steelworker who tops 200 pounds. During a break, the mother approached me and said, "I didn't know she could do that!"

"A few months ago," I nodded, "neither did she."

Over the years, I have heard a number of similar anecdotes from many students—schoolyard bullies converted to admirers, purse-snatchers foiled, would-be assailants stopped in their tracks with a simple technique. And many more who, happily, have not had to use the techniques of Shindo in actual self-defense have related testimonials to the quiet but solid inner confidence and grace acquired by ordinary folks who undertake the extraordinary discipline of investing the time and effort to arm themselves with a sound knowledge of basic self-defense.

Why bother, you may ask, to learn self-defense techniques at all? Wouldn't it be simpler just to carry a gun?

There are many good answers to this question, including the immediately obvious: "What do you do when attacked without your gun?" Police reports are legion in which the bad guy gains control of the gun and then turns it against the owner. Moreover, how much time do you imagine the average mugger will allow you to fumble around in your pocket or handbag, searching for your hardware, before he strikes?

Even assuming that you do manage to discharge your blunderbuss in the general direction of your attacker, what if your bullet misses (or goes through) him and inadvertently hits an innocent bystander?

And then there is the expense, mess, liability, and trouble of maintaining a gun, keeping it loaded, and lugging it around everywhere you go. Do you arm your teenage daughter or son? Your brother or sister?

Husband? Wife? Girl- or boyfriend? Father or mother? If you have kids in the house, you've read horror stories aplenty to know that this is simply an unacceptably hazardous option.

Self-defense training provides a much better, more flexible, and safer option—one that never jams, rusts, or runs out of ammunition, and is with you always.

In addition to presenting practical self-defense information that can work effectively for everyone, as a martial arts instructor I also hope that this book will inspire at least some of our readers to seek out and explore further training in the traditional martial arts. Over many years in the field, I have seen martial arts training provide so much personal confidence, focus, discipline, empowerment, and joy to so many people that I want to share these gifts with as many others as possible.

The martial art of Tao-Zen Ryu Shindo is a relatively recent innovation, but despite differences in emphasis from one martial arts "style" to another, the basic tactics, theories, and philosophies taught in this book are compatible with most other systems of traditional martial arts training. See the Appendix for guidance in finding the right system and school for you.

For the many other readers who, for whatever reasons, are not presently able or inclined to pursue formal study of the martial arts, this book, together with dedicated effort and practice, can provide a sound basic knowledge of the skills, theories, techniques, and tactics required for effective personal defense.

Good luck. Enjoy. Have fun. Grow!

—Master Townsend
Pioneer Hill Dojang
Summer 2005

HOW TO USE THIS BOOK

This book is organized into four main sections:

I. Theory

II. Techniques

III. Applications

IV. Appendices

The first section introduces some of the philosophies that form the basis of the classical martial arts, and of Tao-Zen Ryu Shindo, the Taoist-oriented system upon which this book is based. It also provides the theory that underpins the actual techniques and applications you'll be learning in following sections, enabling you to understand *how* and *why* your techniques work so effectively in self-defense applications, regardless of the size and strength of any attacker.

Section II introduces the concept of your "mental toolbox" and shows you how to stock it with the most useful and accessible "tools" for practical, real-world self-defense. Here are the actual techniques you'll be working with, along with some vital insights into how to maximize the effectiveness of the techniques that work best for you.

Owning a tool and knowing how to use it are two different things. In section III, you'll see how to deploy your tools most effectively in a variety of common self-defense situations.

Section IV provides reference information for those who wish to delve deeper into their self-defense practice or the martial arts generally.

We know you're going to want to skip ahead to the "fun parts," where all the pictures are, and that's fine—hey, it's your book now. *But* (you did see a "but" coming, didn't you?) be sure not to cheat yourself by just going for the pretty wrapping and throwing away the gifts inside.

Can you glance at the pictures and figure out intuitively how a technique works? Superficially, perhaps. But a quick "sneak peek" is not likely to enable you to use the technique effectively and reliably in a variety of defensive situations.

You've heard the old saying that "you get what you pay for," and that is especially true in regard to the time and effort you invest in your martial arts training. Don't deprive yourself of the deeper understanding of the principles that make these techniques work so effectively. Give yourself the time to read and fully understand the information in the other sections as well.

Bear in mind that just reading about a technique won't ensure that it will be there when you need it. Like getting to Carnegie Hall, the secret to truly owning a technique is practice, practice, practice. "Setting Up" in the Techniques section tells you how.

You no doubt noted that this part is titled "How to *Use* This Book" rather than "How to *Read*" it, and if you got a mental whiff of impending exertion, your premonitory senses are working just fine. For those who want to really own reliably workable self-defense tools, some serious sweat-equity is necessarily involved.

You can curl up by the fire with this book for a cozy read and a cup of tea, but don't get too comfortable. The introduction to Theory can be read with your feet up, but later sections on Technique and Applications are designed to be interactive—with the accent on *active*. We'll soon have you hopping up and down like the Dow Jones.

Once you've read through the "sit down" sections and are ready to actually set up your practice space and get going, the book is designed to be an immediately accessible reference and guide. Keep it with you, propped up on a windowsill or other handy spot where you can flip back and forth through the illustrations and instructions as you actually work physically with each technique. Carefully observe your progress in your mirrors, and with a serious, capable, and trustworthy workout partner, if you're lucky (and determined) enough to find one (or more).

Remember that safety comes first, always. Injuring yourself or your training partners rather defeats the purpose of learning self-defense in the first place.

Not that the occasional bump, bruise, or sprain won't happen—they do. Sore muscles now and again are nature's way of saying "no pain, no gain." But if you're breaking bones or driving yourself to serious downtime for injuries, you're going too hard. If a partner is too "gung ho" and won't back things down—if not to your comfort level necessarily, at least to reliable safety—then he or she is not the right partner for you. Training should be sweaty, hard, and *fun*.

How hard and how sweaty? And, for that matter, how much fun? These are all issues of individual taste, and the advantage of working out with this book in your own *dojang* space is that *you* decide how hard to go, with whom, and how often. I recommend every other day as the ideal schedule; one day to work, one day to rest, then back to it.

If you find and join a good school, their schedule will have to be factored into your workout routine. The advantages of working with a good instructor and with the reinforcement of a group are obvious, for those who have the option.

Again, for those who do not presently have the option of a good school and truly qualified instruction, this book will help you build your own personal "toolbox" of effective, workable, real-world self-defense techniques. Let's get going!

I. THEORY

THE TAOIST PERSPECTIVE
IN TRADITIONAL MARTIAL ARTS

Many people associate Taoist thinking with the basic concepts of yin and yang, most elegantly and simply expressed in the ancient symbol for the Tao: ☯

Many are attracted by the fact that Taoism is a philosophy, rather than a religion. Because its powers and mysteries have not been codified into rigid or exclusive ideologies, their exploration and practice remain equally accessible to the open and inquiring minds of all people, everywhere. The principles of Taoist thought and spirit are therefore truly universal.

Taoist theory adopts a broad perspective, encompassing both "sides" of perceived differences, ultimately revealing the essential unity that underlies—and hence, resolves—many of life's seeming contradictions.

This versatility is particularly useful in martial arts and basic self-defense training, and it is used very consciously in the "style" or system of martial art and science called Tao-Zen Ryu Shindo, on which this book is based. This Taoist-oriented martial art is a modern synthesis of the best techniques, tactics, and theories of a number of systems or "styles" of traditional Asian martial arts. In these pages, we will sometimes refer to the system as simply "Shindo."

One of the most important advantages of a Taoist perspective in martial art is the universal effectiveness of its defensive techniques, which work as well for smaller and lighter practitioners as they do for larger and stronger people. This makes Shindo, like other Taoist-oriented martial arts, an ideal system for women, teens, elders, and even children, as well as for men and women in the prime of youth and strength.

Shindo techniques rely on timing, leverage, and blending with the attacker in order to use the aggressor's power to the defender's advantage. This is the reason why with these techniques, relative size and strength truly don't matter. The old adage that "the bigger they are, they harder they fall" is literally true.

EVENING THE ODDS

The Tao-Zen Ryu Shindo system of martial art was specifically created to make *effective* self-defense techniques available to smaller and lighter people: women, teens, older folks, lighter men, and even kids. While other, impact-based styles such as *karate, taekwondo,* and some types of *"kung fu"* work best for natural athletes and young people in their physical prime—especially young men—Shindo works for everyone else also. Using most other systems, the biggest and strongest usually prevail. Not so with Shindo. Consider the analogy of a bull and matador; if they clash head to head, the much larger and stronger bull usually wins.

Transposing that analogy to two humans— a large, powerful attacker, say, and you— wouldn't it be great if, instead of clashing head to head, you had, ready at hand, self-defense tools so powerful that they could instantly neutralize the attacker's size and strength, and instead turn the advantage to you? Well, here's a secret known to martial artists since antiquity: you in fact *do* have such tools, and they in fact *are* with you—always. Shindo shows you many ways to neutralize a larger attacker's size and strength by fighting smarter, instead of harder, using natural weapons you were born with, and techniques like the ones we call "the equalizers."

You'll find not just dozens but scores of "equalizers" in this book—far more than you'll ever need. Let's start with a look at some of the "big gun" concepts, including:

- ☯ Awareness and Avoidance
- ☯ Evasion
- ☯ Full-Body Power
- ☯ Breaking the Root
- ☯ Moving Off the Line of Attack
- ☯ Stealing the Attacker's Power

The basic working theories that make each of these "equalizers" so effective—*regardless of relative size or strength*—are examined in the pages that follow.

Once you understand the theory that underlies each technique, we'll work to practice and develop them into highly effective, instantly available, natural body weapons that you can confidently add to your personal self-defense toolbox.

Keep in mind that knowledge really is power. The more you study and practice the tactics and techniques in this book, the more knowledge you will acquire, the more powerful your equalizers will become, and the more proficient you will be at evening the odds, should ever the need arise.

INTRODUCTION TO THE SHINDO THEORY OF KINETICS

When we learn any complex physical activity, we usually have to start quite consciously, by painstakingly mastering new and unfamiliar motor skills. Consider learning to ride a bicycle. Initially, we look down at the pedals as we push down on them, and at the road immediately beneath and directly before us. We wobble precariously, and probably take a fair share of spills. Should a noise distract us from our intense concentration on pushing the pedals, manipulating the handlebars, and keeping our balance, over we go. In time, however, and with lots of practice, these skills are learned so thoroughly and naturally that we can just hop on the bike and take off, without thinking consciously about the skills we have mastered. We no longer wobble, whizzing along quite confidently, never bothering to glance at the pedals, perhaps even letting go of the handlebars, relaxing and taking in the scenery around us in a leisurely manner, seeing obstacles far ahead, waving and calling greetings to friends and passers-by. We master the skills of bike-riding. We do not forget these skills; the knowledge remains in our mind with every pedal stroke. But we eventually transcend the necessity to think consciously about them, and we simply *do* it; we have learned to ride the bike in a state of *mushin*.

Mushin is an important concept in traditional Japanese martial arts. The term does not translate into English very simply, but a fair approximation might be what is meant by the English phrase "automatic pilot." *Mushin* signifies that one is not relying on conscious thought processes, yet remains fully alert, even "hyper-conscious." An example would be your reaction if a friend unexpectedly yelled, "Think fast!" and suddenly tossed a ball at you. You would instinctively move—faster than the speed of conscious thought—to catch the ball before it hit you. You would not take the time to deliberately consider your response. Like riding a bike, driving a car, or any of the myriad of complex functions we learn to master through experience and practice, you would just *do it,* "automatically"—in a state of *mushin.* Even complex martial art skills such as evasions, blocking, kicking, striking, locks, and throws can become second nature. In each case, we must initially invest the time and work required to achieve a natural "feel" for—and a reliable, instantaneously confident command of—the skills desired.

However deliberately one may practice any given technique, if ever it becomes necessary to use it in a real self-defense situation (or in full-speed sparring), the practitioner will hardly pause to ruminate about how to perform the technique, or to reflect on the kinetic theory underlying. The technique is simply *done,* "automatically" and at a speed far faster than conscious thought.

Achieving this ability takes practice. We can watch a technique just once and "learn" the concept mentally, but to really "own" the technique—what we call "learning in the bones"—takes time and practice. Just like rid-

ing a bike and driving a car, the more effort we invest in mastering those skills, the better we can perform them.

The *tao symbol,* sometimes called the "yin-yang" symbol (☯), is useful in representing and exploring concepts of such complexity and subtlety that their verbal explication is often too clumsy, involved, or imprecise to efficiently express the idea. This ancient and universal symbol reminds us of the essential unity that underlies all of the seeming paradoxes presented by the apparent duality of our universe.

More than just the representation of obvious phenomena, such as light and dark, good and bad, hot and cold, male and female, and so on, the *tao* symbol reminds us also of more abstract concepts, and of subtler contrasts. A prime example from the field of martial arts is the long-established fact that knowledge can be at once dismissed from conscious thought and yet, simultaneously, be fully present within us at every moment, in every breath, and with each step that we take. Once properly learned, this knowledge can be immediately accessed at any time—directly, without having to pause for conscious reflection.

The Shindo General Theory of Kinetics examines the fundamental physics underlying some of the basic martial arts techniques used in real-world self-defense situations. In order for the ensuing discussion to make much sense, however, it will first be necessary to introduce a few basic concepts and items of terminology central to the thesis. Several of these terms and concepts are referred to only briefly at the beginning of the section, and are explored in more detail further into the work.

Whole-Body Movement

Traditionally, a great deal of emphasis is placed on the proper deployment of weapons (e.g. hands, feet, elbows, knees, and so on). In many—but not all—styles, the *coordination of these movements with the rest of the body* is eventually taught, but only at relatively advanced levels. Because the techniques used in Shindo have been developed and refined with smaller and lighter practitioners specifically in mind, this fundamental concept is taught right from the beginning. Without such coordination, only the isolated power of the individual weapon (hand, arm, leg, etc.) is used, instead of the combined and coordinated power of the whole body. This is the reason that the concept of *whole-body movement* (also referred to as *whole-body power*) is integral to so many of the techniques used in Tao-Zen Ryu Shindo, and in many other traditional martial arts.

T'an T'ien

T'an t'ien is a Chinese term referring to the center of gravity in the human body. While this is a gross oversimplification of the meaning of *t'an t'ien* (rhymes, more or less, with the English word "dungeon"), it will suffice for the purposes of the basics presented in this book. The importance of the concept of *t'an t'ien* cannot be overemphasized. Western readers not raised with the concept of *t'an t'ien* as a cultural given may be tempted to dismiss it as an intellectual abstraction. To those who take the time and trouble to pursue it, however, it will, in time and with practice, become a very tangibly felt physical reality. Some find it right away; for others it may take weeks, months, or even years. Persevere—this fundamental feeling is the foundation for your stability, your "root" in all martial art and self-defense performance. If it takes a while for you to find your *t'an t'ien,* do not despair, for you can at least begin to learn and practice martial art and self-defense, working with the mental concept alone. Above all, do not become discouraged and give up; the concepts that are initially the most elusive often develop into the very ones that are most solidly understood, once they are ultimately mastered. The *t'an t'ien* location is illustrated in a line drawing in the "Centerline" section further into this chapter.

Foot-Pound

This engineering term describes the amount of energy required to move one pound of mass the distance of one foot through space (usually in the direction of the force applied). The foot-pound in this context is used as a handy unit of measurement to analyze, design, refine, and express the relative force and power involved at the point of contact by the various physical techniques examined in Shindo kinetic theory.

A.C.T.

This mnemonic acronym is used to describe the method by which whole-body movement is incorporated into each technique, thereby ensuring that maximum power is developed by the movement(s) performed.

Shindo techniques use the power of the whole body in order to generate maximum power. The transmission of power flows from A, the anchor, through C, the center *(t'an t'ien)*, and is then projected out through T, the target, which is contacted by the hand (or other body weapon).

The entire line of power, running from the anchor to the point at which force is issued at the target, is called the *ACT trajectory,* or more simply, the *line of power.*

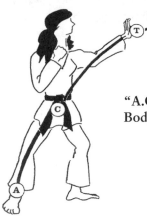

"A.C.T." and Whole-Body Power

Centerline

The concept of the *centerline* is crucial in martial arts generally, and especially in Shindo. It may be regarded as a straight line running through the middle of the spine (i.e., your central nervous system). Please refer to the expanded discussion of Centerline, and accompanying illustration, a bit later in this chapter.

Breaking the Root

Maintaining a strong stance and destroying the balance of your attacker are fundamentally important skills that are often key in determining who wins and who loses in any physical confrontation.

So important is this technique that in some traditional schools during the classical times of yesteryear, a single stance *(kiba dachi,* the horse stance, used to teach this single skill) was the sole technique taught for the first six months of training. To get a sense of the dedication required of martial arts students in those days and in those schools, skip ahead to the discussion of stances in the Techniques section, find the horse stance, and try it out. Start with one minute, then quit and see how your legs feel. Imagine doing that and that only—for fifteen minutes or more at a time—for six months. Few students in the modern day would have that kind of discipline, but you can bet those guys were pretty hard to tip over!

Armed with these few basic concepts and the relevant terminology, we are ready to proceed with our examination of Shindo kinetic theory. Bear in mind as we work with the concepts (and later with the actual techniques and applications) that these theories are the foundation that underpins and supports the effectiveness of your techniques.

Like learning to ride the bicycle, it will at first require deliberate effort to keep all of these concepts in mind, and to incorporate them all into each technique. Over time, however, and with practice, this knowledge will "sink into the bones," and you will find yourself performing your techniques with grace, speed, and power, almost effortlessly, incorporating and applying all of these theories and concepts "automatically"—in a state of *mushin*.

There are two basic kinds of fighters: amateur street thugs and bullies, and trained martial artists.

If you learn and practice the techniques taught in this book and use them only under the conditions specified herein, then you fall into the second category; you are a martial artist.

The principal characteristics distinguishing martial artists from untrained combatants include careful study and thought, regular and diligent practice, and a strong code of personal honor.

FORCE AND POWER

Shindo kinetic theory draws on a Taoist perspective to recognize a fundamental distinction between the concepts of *force* and *power*.

Just as ice and water are the same material in two distinctly different forms and conditions, Shindo regards the concepts of force and power as two different expressions of energy.

Because Shindo is a martial art, these considerations are usually expressed in the context of physical interaction—usually confrontation or conflict between attacker(s) and defender(s).

Force is regarded as physical energy exerted by an individual (usually, at least initially, the attacker).

Power is regarded as energy "borrowed" or co-opted from other sources, such as the attacker's force, and then redirected and/or amplified by leverage, timing, and environmental factors, often at the direction of the defender.

Because the techniques of Tao-Zen Ryu Shindo are specifically designed to be effective for smaller and lighter defenders, those employing Shindo defensive techniques usually try to employ *power* rather than rely on *force*.

In light of these considerations, it quickly becomes clear that power will usually be able to overcome force precisely because the incoming energy is redirected and used to defeat itself.

Making this all work in real life, of course, requires considerable skill—which is what all that practice is about. The kind of practice undertaken by serious students of martial art—and basic self-defense—is precisely the "magic" that can transform the merely martial into true *art*.

One can spin endless analogies: the force of the charging bull met with the last-second evasive skill of the matador; the attempted punch or grab redirected by a smaller defender who uses the incoming force to defeat the attack, and so on. In each case, the physical force of the larger and stronger attacker is successfully met by smaller defenders who use the incoming energy to generate seemingly effortless power, thus effectively—even artfully—resolving the situation.

As Grandmaster Yun never tired of telling us: when pulled, follow; when pushed, yield. In this way, the Taoist perspectives of Shindo kinetic theory have endless defensive applications. Meet hard with soft; yang with yin. Don't bother wasting valuable time or energy; if an opponent insists on providing force, simply accept and then convert it to your own ends to develop and direct the power required to resolve the situation.

Appreciate the value of both hard, rigid ice and soft, fluid water. Understand that they are at once different and the same. Practice toward the day when you can move effortlessly between them, like fog.

YOUR PERSONAL SPACE: *MAAI* AND THE SPHERE OF INFLUENCE

We all need a certain amount of personal space in which we feel comfortable and secure. How large or small this space may be changes according to cultural norms, personal preference, and, in the context of self-defense, situational circumstances.

Imagine, for a moment, a lover or very close friend. How close would you like to have that person to you? Now imagine a very casual acquaintance, perhaps a co-worker you don't know well. How close would you like to have that person? Now imagine a total stranger on the street, perhaps acting erratically or even threateningly. How close would you want that person to get to you? Clearly the range of distance—and relative level of caution—differs depending on the person and the circumstances of the situation.

This idea of "personal space" is so universally understood in human interaction that most of us never give it a conscious thought, and many languages don't even have a specific word to describe it. In martial arts, however, and for the purposes of formal study of self-defense, it is useful to have some term of reference for this concept. Let us use the term *"circle (or sphere) of influence"* as a handy way to refer to this principle.

Japanese martial artists have long referred to this concept using the term *maai* ("mah-eye"), which translates roughly into English as "distancing."

Correct *maai* may be understood, in very basic terms, as maintaining a safe distance between you and an attacker. More advanced practitioners would refine this definition to include other factors, such as maintaining a distance (and stance) that keeps you safe from attack but also keeps you close enough to quickly deliver an effective counter.

We can visualize our personal *circle of influence* as a circle on the ground and imagine ourselves standing safely in its center.

If we expand our space to three dimensions, we can envision our circle becoming our personal *sphere* of influence.

Some might prefer the mental imagery of a bubble, or a beach ball.

Since it's your space, you are free to imagine it in any way you like. The idea is to keep in mind some convenient visualization of your personal space, into which you invite those you welcome, and from which you exclude those you don't.

At the risk of restating the obvious, it is worth reinforcing here the fact that *no one has the right to enter your personal space without your permission.* If everyone understood and honored this simple truth, there would be no need for this book, and no need to learn self-defense. Alas, however, there are still people out there who just don't get it, and it behooves us to be ready for any situations that may arise in which someone does attempt to enter our sphere without welcome.

In self-defense, any unwelcome attempt to enter our personal sphere is called an *attack*. While there are many possible kinds of attack, the vast majority fall into a few common types. For purposes of easy reference, we divide them into three main categories: *Strikes, Captures,* and *Groundwork*. These are all examined in greater detail in the Applications section of this book.

Attacks can also vary widely in seriousness, from unintentional accidents to careless horseplay and overly "friendly" overtures, to outright life-threatening assaults. Developing your ability to quickly perceive, correctly assess, and instantly respond to such incursions is a critically important skill in basic self-defense.

Throughout this book, and as you go about your daily life, the key concept to keep in mind is the idea of your personal space—your *circle or sphere of influence*—and your right (indeed, your responsibility) to maintain its integrity. Strive to develop and maintain a continual, comfortable awareness in all situations. Stay alert, stay relaxed, and stay safe inside your personal *sphere of influence*.

T'AN T'IEN, BREATHING, AND CH'I

T'an t'ien is a Chinese term for which there is no precise equivalent in English. The same concept is expressed by the Japanese word *hara*. English speakers generally pronounce *t'an t'ien* to sound more or less like "dungeon," which, if one accents the second syllable, will probably be close enough to get by. Basically, the term refers to the center of gravity in the human body, located in the center of the lower abdomen. *T'an t'ien* is also regarded as the point of connection between the physical and spiritual planes, and many traditional schools of martial art teach that all physical movement (includ-

ing breathing) proceeds from—and returns to—this central point.

To locate your *t'an t'ien*, stand comfortably and spread your fingers wide. Place your index finger on your navel, palm facing in, and press your widely spread fingers down the front of your abdomen. Where your third or ring finger rests, reinforce the pressure with your other hand, pressing gently in as you breathe out deeply. Imagine that you are breathing out not only from your chest or stomach but all the way from *t'an t'ien*, in the center of your lower abdomen.

Now bend your knees a bit, feet slightly wider than shoulder-width apart. Breathing out, take a sliding step forward and then back, and then, perhaps, to each side, gliding lightly so that your feet never quite leave the ground. Keeping your knees slightly bent and your weight low, mentally envision and physically feel yourself generating the energy for each move, and each breath, from your *t'an t'ien*. As you envision the in-breath traveling up through your nasal passages, up over the crown of your head, and then down your spine, let it draw your chin up, your shoulders back and down, and your posture erect. Keep your back straight, and tuck your tail a bit in and under. Grip the ground firmly with your feet.

Hold the breath tightly coiled in *t'an t'ien* for a moment, and then imagine the tight spiral uncoiling from the *t'an t'ien* spot and back out again. As you exhale, press in on the front of your abdomen in order to help you visualize and "feel" the *t'an t'ien* spot. Moving about in wide, slow, gliding steps, imagine the out-breath flowing up the front of your torso and out through your mouth. You may find it helpful to purse your lips slightly to slow the out-breath, but not so tightly that you produce a whistling sound. Keep all tension low, in *t'an t'ien,* relaxing your tongue, jaw, neck, shoulders, arms, back, and legs. Lower your eyelids to "half mast," and smile gently. You are breathing to and from, moving from, and focusing your concentration in the center of gravity in your body—your *t'an t'ien.*

Breathing to and from *t'an t'ien* focuses your attention and calms your mind, both in motion and in stillness. Moving from *t'an t'ien* imparts power and stability to your movement, centering and balancing your body, and keeping your weight low. Transmitting power through (and back to) *t'an t'ien* in the performance of your martial art self-defense techniques maximizes available power.

When the doctor whacks us on the back as newborns, we begin breathing with a yell, and most of us never give breathing a second thought thereafter. For the martial artist, however, breathing is a critically conscious exercise. Proper instruction in the correct tech-

niques of deep breathing requires the direct supervision of a qualified instructor, but it is enough for the student of basic self-defense simply to be aware that deep (and conscious) breathing—from *t'an t'ien*—is important to his or her ability to perform well under the stress of rigorous training or in the heat of any actual self-defense situation that may arise.

Particularly useful in developing deep breathing is the Shindo exercise called "Crushing the Barrel." To perform this exercise, stand with the feet somewhat wider than shoulder-width apart, relaxed. Inhale slowly and deeply through your nose as you raise your arms in front of your body, crossing them in front of your face and then opening them out as they rise above your head. Continue to inhale and open your arms down and out to your sides at shoulder level, palms up. Raise your chin and close, or nearly close, your eyes.

IN   **OUT**

Envision and feel the progress of the air as you follow a mental image of the air flowing in a circuit up your nasal passages, over the top of your brain, and then down your neck and spine, straightening your back as it flows down to your tailbone and into *t'an t'ien*.

Hold your full inspiration in *t'an t'ien* for a moment, and then begin to exhale slowly, your chin relaxing down onto your chest, your stomach pushing gently *out* (not in). Turn your palms forward, down, and inward toward your lower abdomen. Creating tension in your arms and all muscles from your neck down to your toes, mentally envision the air uncoiling from *t'an t'ien,* rising up the inside of your torso and out through your mouth. Imagine that you are crushing a giant plastic barrel or a large beach ball into a small wad as you lower your arms, bringing your hands down to face your lower abdomen, toward *t'an t'ien.* Purse your lips slightly to slow the egress of air.

As you complete the exhale, relax all muscle groups and shake out your arms and hands to discharge any remaining energy and tension. Let your chin relax completely onto your chest, your shoulders slumping comfortably forward and arms dangling loosely at your sides, relaxing as completely as you can without actually falling down. In Shindo classes, this relaxation phase is called "Marionette on Slack Strings" (or, more simply, "Broken Puppet"), which

gives a fair mental image of the feeling desired. The entire exercise should be performed from three to ten times each day, and it serves as a great "stress buster" any time.

We have examined this exercise in minute detail precisely because *breathing* is such a vital element in martial arts, and in self-defense. Regular deep breathing enhances health, vitality, endurance, energy, and general ability to perform well. It enables you to better control your breathing (and your emotional response) in situations of special demand, such as escape from danger, fighting (perhaps with more than one assailant), and quick recovery from other highly aerobic and/or emergency exertions.

It is a crucial point in correct breathing technique to be sure to breathe *out* when executing a technique, or receiving a blow. This is the same principle observed when one unconsciously exclaims "oof!" with an accompanying expulsion of air when lifting something heavy, or when getting poked in the stomach. This is also the principle behind the powerful shouts often used by martial artists during practice and sparring. Breathing out is nature's way of protecting you from internal injury in such circumstances. Conversely, breathing in or holding the breath when receiving a blow or delivering a powerful technique can be very dangerous. Protect yourself, and enhance your power: breathe strongly *out* under these conditions.

Ch'i, also spelled Ki or Qi, and variously

pronounced "chee," "jee," or "key," is an almost mystical force anciently regarded as a naturally occurring form of energy which links the realms and dimensions of the physical and spiritual.

Ch'i is nurtured in the human body and most directly accessed through the *t'an t'ien,* or *hara,* and it is directed and controlled by conscious breathing and the informed intention of those trained in traditional martial arts—and in basic self-defense.

Is a working understanding of and reliable feel for *ch'i* elusive? Yes. Is it subtle? Yes. Difficult to develop? For most of us, yes—very. An advanced concept, it requires the luck of finding a truly qualified instructor (very rare in this day), and even then, a great deal of patience and practice. Is it really worth all that trouble to acquire? Absolutely. Is it necessary for basic self-defense? No, but the concept is sufficiently important that you should be at least aware that it exists, and that it is available to anyone with the discipline and determination to seek it out.

Many books on this subject, by sages far wiser than this writer, have for ages informed not only the martial arts community but also those whose wisdom extends to respect for and curiosity about longevity, vitality, and the more holistic health achievable only when the energies of body, mind, and spirit are in harmony.

Authentic masters of traditional martial arts have taught for centuries that true strength comes not from muscular force alone, but by aligning and investing one's breathing, intention, and techniques with the cosmic power of *ch'i.*

CENTERLINE

The centerline of the human body is a concept of crucial importance in the martial arts. Just like it sounds, it is an imaginary line that runs straight down the center of your spine. When you are standing, you can imagine this line extending down between your legs directly to the earth. In fact, it is helpful to imagine this line as running clear to the center of the earth, "rooting" your body with immense firmness

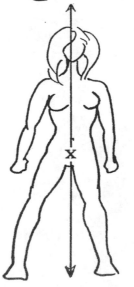

Centerline

to the ground. This concept is at the heart of an important technique that the Chinese call "breaking the root." Refer to that section of this book for more detail.

You can also envision this line as extending upward from the top of your head to the heavens, and many traditional Chinese schools teach that one's posture should be upright, "as if the head were suspended from the ceiling by a string." The idea is to maintain erect posture and, simultaneously, a strong "root."

The most effective stances in martial arts are all designed to protect the centerline. Along this line, just below the level of your hips, resides your center of gravity. This point, denoted by the "X" in the illustration, is the *t'an t'ien*.

You can take a hit or even sustain fairly severe injury to your limbs and outlying areas of your body, and survive. Strikes to the centerline, however, endanger vital organs, and its protection is therefore paramount.

The crisp "snap" of the techniques of experienced martial artists results precisely from this consideration: an extended arm or leg opens the centerline to attack, and the seasoned practitioner seeks to strike and return to "ready" position, guarding the centerline, as quickly as possible.

LINE OF ATTACK

Most attacks are directed in a straight line from the attacker to the intended victim. The best defense against any attack is *not to be there* when it arrives. Therefore, the first principle

TIP: A sudden *Crescent Step* to the side is a quick, easy, and effective way to get off the line of attack!

of defense in Shindo is to *move off the line of attack*. This can be accomplished in many ways: a quick turn, step, pivot, or jump—even a simple twist, lean, or dodge can sometimes work. (Refer to the section on Crescent Steps.) Whether the attack misses by a mile, a block, or an inch doesn't matter; any miss will do.

This initial tactic places the defender momentarily out of harm's way—and for a trained martial artist, a moment is all that is needed to launch a defensive counter. Moreover, any block or other counter-attack is far more effective from an unexpected position to the attacker's side.

BREAKING THE ROOT

One of the many ideas and terms that Shindo has borrowed from our Chinese ancestors is the concept of "breaking (or maintaining) the root." The root, in this colorful connotation, is one's balance—yours and/or that of your opponent.

The importance of balance is clearly demonstrated by assuming a strong stance and having a partner try to push you over. Then repeat the exercise while standing on one leg.

Even Hercules would be easily toppled if his balance were destroyed.

The preferred situation, of course, is to strongly maintain your own root (balance) and at the same time to break the root of your opponent by somehow compromising, upsetting, or destroying his or her balance.

Imagine the biggest, strongest mugger standing on one leg; you could easily push him over using just one finger. Breaking the opponent's root is one of the key defensive techniques in turning the size and power of larger aggressors to the advantage of smaller defenders.

There are many ways to break the root of an attacker. The foundation, however, is to work on developing a strong root in all of your own stances, and in maintaining that strong root when in transition between stances, or under attack.

Keys to keeping a strong root for yourself, and breaking that of your opponent, include:

- Keep your weight low, in *t'an t'ien*. Resist the temptation to let your weight "float," or rise to your shoulders.

- Keep your hips and shoulders in a straight line; do not twist or torque at the waist, shoulders, or knees. In Shindo, we practice moving about with a *bo* (staff) held across our hips and also over the shoulders, arms draped over the *bo,* in the manner used to carry water buckets in olden times. An instructor who might tell you to "Carry the water!" is reminding you not to twist at the waist.

- As you and your opponent move about, be sure that you always move in such a way as to maintain the straight line of your hips and shoulders, avoiding any twisting or turning from the waist, shoulders, or knees. A good way to do this is to use Crescent Steps.

- Humans are bipeds; we stand on two legs. This arrangement is handily exploited in upsetting the balance ("breaking the root") of an opponent. Maintain continual awareness of the positioning of your opponent's feet, and lead his or her weight off the line between their feet—i.e., push or pull, lead, or otherwise entice them to move at an angle perpendicular to the line between their feet (a 90° angle is best).

AWARENESS AND AVOIDANCE

The best fights, like the best car wrecks, are the ones you don't get into. When you first learned to drive a car, your concentration was initially focused closely on the steering wheel and other controls, eventually expanding beyond the dashboard to the car immediately ahead. In time, as you began driving with more confidence and less conscious effort (i.e., in a state of *mushin*, as explained in the Shindo Theory of Kinetics section), you relaxed and broadened your field of attention to what was happening fifty and then a hundred feet or more ahead. On a highway, experienced drivers observe road conditions a quarter- or half-mile ahead or more, scanning the roadway for potential problems. This is *defensive* driving. Defensive drivers don't get involved in as many accidents as do drivers who are less attentive. Precisely the same principles apply in other defensive situations as well.

Those who look ahead and move defensively are able to anticipate and avoid problems more readily than those whose attention doesn't extend much beyond the end of their own nose. It is far easier to avoid problems before they arise than to battle your way out of situations that, with a bit more vigilance, need not develop in the first place. When waiting at a crosswalk for the light to change, for example, consider positioning your back against a light pole or mailbox, making yourself less easily accessible from behind. While jogging along a country road, it takes but a moment to snap a glance back over your shoulder to make sure that the driver who just passed you is in fact continuing on his way.

Always enter any room—and for that matter, any situation—in an aware state; don't just blindly blunder into a potential for unpleasant surprise.

Training for self-defense involves the mind as well as the body. One very useful—and enjoyable—mental exercise, easily and inconspicuously incorporated into the ordinary activities of daily life, is the *"What's Happening?"* game. As you go about routine affairs—getting on a bus, entering a restaurant, negotiating a darkened parking lot, using a cash machine, and so on—ask yourself; *"What's happening*—right here, right now?" Quickly analyze each situation, and then proceed in a comfortably relaxed but continually alert mode. If you sense trouble brewing, simply take evasive action. Is there a group of rowdy drunks hanging around the ATM you want to use? Can you use another one down the street, or come back to this one later? Is there a chair-hurling riot in progress in the restaurant where you intended to have lunch? Perhaps another café would be a better choice this time. Don't care for the looks of the gang headed down the street toward you? Cross the street, or enter a store until they pass by.

Old martial artists get that way because they avoid unnecessary conflict whenever honorably possible. In self-defense, an ounce of prevention is worth far more than a pound of cure. The keys are **awareness** and **avoidance.**

EVASION: WHEN AVOIDANCE FAILS

The best defense against even the most powerful attack is also the simplest: *don't be there when it arrives!* This obvious truth is the basis for many of the most effective defensive fighting techniques. You really don't need to care how powerful your opponent's attack is, as long as it misses you; nor does it matter whether the miss is by an inch or a mile. The point is that you don't get hit. Bruce Lee had a modern phrase for this ancient technique; he referred to it as "target denial."

Ducking, dodging, or "slipping," stepping back or, better yet, to the side, and sometimes even stepping *directly in toward* an opponent are all possible ways of causing an intended blow to miss you, or of mitigating its impact.

Other methods of achieving the same goals include blocking or redirecting the blow, and, of course, the perhaps less elegant but nevertheless very effective tactic of walking or running away.

In the case of split-second evasions during actual confrontations, one of the most useful tactics is a quick side step. While a step straight back may gain a little distance from an incoming attack, it is often not enough and still leaves you directly in the "line of fire." Better to get entirely off that line of attack as quickly as you can. A quick side step, or better yet, a crescent step, is frequently the best option, and this technique positions you ideally to launch an effective counter-attack.

Practice at moving *quickly* is crucial to the development of effective evasion skills.

Facing your mirror in the ready position, practice these moves against your workout partner or imaginary opponent: never relaxing your guard, keeping your elbows in and hands up in proper ready stance, glide forward and back in a straight line with your partner (or your image in the mirror). Have your training partner (or mirror opponent) throw jabs, punches, and kicks as you advance and retreat. Alternate blocks and ducking responses with *quick, sudden* crescent steps to the side—left, right, in (toward your opponent), and out (back and away)—so that the incoming attacks just miss, like a bull rushing past a matador. Award yourself a mental *Olé!* each time your evasive speed improves significantly. Be prepared, following every evasion, to follow up with an *immediate* counter-attack. These usually succeed, for several reasons: you have seized the initiative, gaining the element of surprise, and you have placed yourself, very quickly, at a right angle to the line of the intended attack. Your opponent's attention, power, and momentum are all focused along this line—and *not* on the space into which you have suddenly and unexpectedly shifted.

IMPROVING YOUR PEOPLE-READING SKILLS

When the opponent attacks, the defender is already in motion to meet him.

—Ancient Chinese maxim

Obviously, you already know how to read books, or we wouldn't be having this conversation. In the martial arts, however, and in order to better handle any physical confrontation, you'll want to expand your observational and interpretive skills to include the ability to "read" people as well.

Simply, we're talking about two different kinds of language. Reading books requires the ability to interpret *written* language, and reading people involves skills in observing and correctly interpreting *body* language.

Just as we had to spend a good deal of time and practice developing our ability to read written language, so it will be necessary to invest some time and effort into learning to read the language of the body.

While there are many written languages, the "body language" of human kinetics is virtually universal. A friendly nod in Walla Walla is a friendly nod in Timbuktu; a punch in Paris is a punch in Singapore. A reader from another culture might hand you a book that would be incomprehensible to you; but an attacker from any culture on Earth will move in pretty much the same way as any other. Learn to read body language, and you'll be ready to deal effectively with attackers anywhere.

Experienced martial artists and seasoned fighters know the importance of developing skills in reading an opponent's intentions, and the equally important skill of not betraying their own. Letting an opponent know your intention ahead of time is called "telegraphing," and martial artists train assiduously to avoid doing so.

Telegraphing—and how to avoid it—are really arts for the ring, however, and not for the street. Street thugs, generally untrained, aren't going to be expecting any effective defense from you and so will not be looking to "read" your intentions. Likewise, such dim bulbs are usually not even going to be aware of the concept of telegraphing, let alone bothering to try to hide their own intentions, and they should therefore be pretty easy subjects for you to read. By all means, learn to do so— it will give you a significant edge in formulating and initiating your responses. Because real-world attacks happen very quickly, any portion of a second can lend a significant—even decisive—edge to your defensive response.

If you are lucky enough to have training partners—either in a school or in your private *dojang*—work on light "tap" or easy "grab" drills, moving around to make it real, blocking as you go, and taking turns trying to "read" your partner's intention. You'll find that, with practice, you will develop the ability to see moves coming sooner, and therefore be "already in motion to meet them."

OPEN-HAND TECHNIQUES

While Shindo practitioners also use the standard closed-fist punches traditional in many styles (although usually in side-fist hammer blocking applications), we emphasize a variety of open-hand techniques, for several reasons.

Greater Safety: The bones of the phalanges (fingers and knuckles) are comparatively small and lightly protected, and they can be easily broken, dislocated, sprained, and otherwise injured, particularly on contact with hard surfaces. In contrast, the hand bones employed in palm-heel and other open-handed strikes (e.g. scaphoids, lunates, capitates, and others) are stronger, and they are surrounded by tougher muscles and ligaments. They can more safely be employed to deliver blows of greater force, with less chance of injury to the practitioner.

Greater Power: The musculoskeletal mechanics of *full body* power and the footwork required to deliver effective open-hand strikes (see "Crescent Steps" in the Techniques section) employ stances conducive to delivery of blows with greater power. (See "Carry the Water" in the Techniques section.)

Greater Speed: Open-hand techniques are quicker than closed-fist blows because the relaxed muscles are more responsive and are not working against the resistance of tensed opposing muscles.

Greater Versatility: Closed-fist techniques may be used for only a relatively few basic punches and blocks. Open-hand techniques lend themselves to a wide variety of useful follow-up moves such as blocks, counter-captures and controls, redirections, and others. Many more hand weapons can be formed, and much more quickly, with open hands.

Enhanced Relaxation: Open hands promote calmer breathing, smoother and quicker movement, less tension, and more relaxed alertness. Try shadow boxing for a minute or so with fists tightly clenched and see how you feel. Then repeat the exercise with hands open and compare breathing and relaxation.

Qi Flow: *Qi* flows much more freely when the hands are open, allowing for better movement and projection of *qi* through your techniques.

Be aware that open-hand techniques require more practice to perform safely than closed-fist blocks. "Open fingers, broken fingers" is an old caution against attempting to block heavy incoming kicks or punches with open hands until one has mastered the art of side-stepping incoming blows and countering with open-hand blocks from a position of temporary relative safety from the side. Be sure to carefully study "Crescent Steps" in the Theory section, and practice exhaustively with them in this connection.

SITUATIONALLY APPROPRIATE RESPONSE

You don't need a sledgehammer to kill a mosquito. Consider these situations:

1. On the street, someone you don't know starts yelling at you, perhaps using obscene language. What is your response?

2. Someone comes up to you at a party and starts fondling you. What is your response?

3. Someone has attacked you in a parking lot, pinning you against a car and trying to choke you with both hands. What is your response?

In the first case, for instance, the person yelling at you may be crazy, drunk, or otherwise impaired. While their behavior is certainly rude, it is not an immediate threat to your physical safety and may require no response beyond leaving the area or simply ignoring them (while keeping an eye on them to be sure they aren't getting closer or escalating to physical assault).

In the case of someone getting "fresh" at a party, your response will probably depend to some extent on who the person is; if it's a good friend, for example, your response will likely be different than if the fondler is a complete stranger. Is the person merely a sloppy drunk or a consciously, deliberately aggressive jerk? A simple admonishment may suffice or, *depending on the situation,* stronger measures such as a slap, a momentary finger lock, or even a knee to the groin may be required. The key phrase here is *depending on the situation.*

How about scenario #3? Your options here are apparently limited; you are going to have to put some serious hurt on this individual, and quickly. You might, in a worst-case situation, even have to kill them in order to save your own life.

The key consideration is that your response will vary according to the circumstances in each individual case. Having a good command of martial art self-defense techniques allows you to tailor an appropriate response to any situation.

Do you rip someone's arm off at the elbow and beat them with the stump because they grabbed your butt at a party? That might be a little strong. While such rude behavior might offend you, you can probably come up with a response that is more *appropriate to that situation*.

Similarly, if someone is trying to rip your clothes off (without your permission), an admonishment and a slap probably won't handle the situation; and again, you can unload a response that is more *situationally appropriate*.

This book will equip you with a wide selection of tools and techniques, which you will carry with you in your "mental toolbox" everywhere you go.

You are therefore prepared always—ready 24 hours a day, 365 days a year—for any situation that may arise.

Be sure that you always use those tools wisely, compassionately, and *appropriately to the situation*.

PERSEVERANCE

Because we all have different aptitudes, affinities, and natural abilities, each of us has different areas that come relatively easily, and, on the flip side, we all face areas that are a bit tougher for us—sometimes enormously so. Some might need to work harder on flexibility; others might have to work harder on forms, or judos, or whatever.

The toughest hurdle for most who aspire to learn self-defense and to follow the martial way is also the obstacle that separates those who successfully achieve self-defense skills and the "wannabees" who only read, talk, and dream about it. That test is *perseverance*. Those who overcome all other difficulties—and there are many—are those who are also able to do the hardest thing and overcome the toughest obstacle of all—inertia.

We've all heard the old joke about excuses (everybody's got one), but excuses don't cut it in training for self-defense.

Everyone, including the most dedicated martial artist, needs a little time off now and again. Life happens, things come up. But do you take "breaks" from training only every now and again, or do you fail to show up for practice whenever it's merely inconvenient?

We all have days when we really, *really* don't feel like working out. The true martial artists—and those who are most successful at acquiring reliable self-defense skills—are the ones who pull it together and show up anyway, and put their best effort into practice, perhaps precisely *because* they don't feel like it today. This is personal discipline, that rare quality that builds the exceptional character of the true martial artist, and of the warrior spirit who achieves the most reliable command and control of self-defense techniques.

One of the secrets that martial artists and other athletes understand is the hidden power of *endorphins*—natural hormones that your body produces when you work hard. Are you feeling today like road kill looks? Sorry to hear it. But, unless you are seriously, doctor's-office ill, you might be surprised to find that a good hard workout will actually leave you feeling much better than you did before you went. This is what athletes refer to as nature's "endorphin high." The real bonus, however, is the personal discipline you gain by showing up and working out *despite* the fact that you felt sub-par to begin with.

So, what's the hardest part of self-defense training? Simply *doing it*. Consistently. Relentlessly. Day in, day out, week in, week out; month after month, year after year after year. If someone led you to believe that martial arts training could be quick or easy, they lied. And if quick and easy are big values for you, you should know right up front that the path of the real martial arts is a long, long way from either. For those, however, who are not quitters, and who are not content to settle for the merely quick and easy, the ancient path of the true warrior offers rewards known only to the few who are willing to "do the do," and *persevere*.

II. TECHNIQUES

TECHNIQUES:
THE TOOLS OF THE TRADE

The Introduction, Theory, and reference sections comprise the "sit-down" portion of this book. However, this section and the next, covering Techniques and Applications, are designed to be physically interactive. Along with our reading, it's time to get moving too.

Book learning is relatively quick; we can mentally grasp general principles in minutes. But kinetically integrating new ways of moving—what we call "learning in the bones"—takes practice, and lots of it. This book is written specifically for people who may not have the time to pursue formal training, and it is important to note that progress in the traditional martial arts can take years. You certainly don't have to shave your head and join a monastery to learn basic self-defense, but you cannot expect to develop any realistic command of even the simplest physical self-defense techniques by merely reading a book—any book—alone. If you really want to "own" even a few effective self-defense moves, some physical effort is required. As Master Yun used to tell us, "More sweat, more better!"

So, as we explore various techniques, we'll ask you to read about them first—and then hop up and actually try them out.

The pictures in this book will guide you; your mirror (and, if you're lucky enough to find good ones, your training partners and teachers) will help you to refine your technique as your practice progresses.

As is true in any other area of life, much of the real work happens between your ears; and many of the exercises we'll be working with will be as much mental as physical. Tao-Zen Ryu Shindo has been called "the thinking man's martial art," and we do strive to "fight smarter, not harder." Don't get too comfortable, however; most of our mental exercises are followed immediately by (or better yet, occur simultaneously with) physical follow-through.

Imagining any technique is one thing; actually doing it is quite another. When, in the section on stances, for example, you read about envisioning the difference between your posture when reaching for an item on a high shelf, and your position when bracing to help push a stalled car, you will be invited to physically adopt those postures. Not in the bookstore, perhaps, but when you get back to the privacy of your own home or *dojang,* go for it.

That said, let's get busy building your personal "mental toolbox," from which you will soon be able to pull your favorite physical tools of effective self-defense instantaneously, if ever the need arises.

BUILDING YOUR SELF-DEFENSE TOOLBOX

We hope you'll never need to use anything you learn in this book in real life (for the bad guys' sake!), because the techniques, tactics, and applications can do some real damage. But it's far better to have effective self-defense tools at the ready and never need them than the other way around.

The concept of a self-defense toolbox is a very useful analogy; and, because the "tools" are ideas and concepts that you carry in your head, they have many advantages over lugging an arsenal of physical hardware everywhere you go.

You can customize your self-defense toolbox by picking and choosing the techniques—the "tools" of self-defense—that work best for you.

As you build your toolbox and stock it with

the techniques you learn, remember that the more you practice, the more effectively and confidently you will be able to access them—anytime, anywhere, *instantly.*

Your mental toolbox is invisible, so no one knows you have it but you. You never have to go looking for it; it's with you always. It can't be lost, stolen, or taken from you and the tools then turned against you by the bad guys—a real danger with physical weapons like knives, guns, and the like. There's no danger of tragic accidents like the kids finding hardware weapons to "play" with. No licenses or permits are required. These tools never wear out or break.

You have much greater control over where and how much force to use, and no worries about hurting innocent bystanders, or accidental discharge if you drop it.

These tools cause no embarrassing alarms in airports, or unsightly lumps and wrinkles in your clothing.

Do be sure, however, to pull your tools out regularly for practice in order to keep them sharp, well-oiled, and ready for use if ever they should be needed.

SETTING UP

Even students lucky enough to belong to a good school should not neglect private practice time on their own, and for students who do not presently have access to a proper school, private practice is their only option. In either case, personal practice space is essential to real progress in any serious study of martial art and self-defense.

Nothing really worth having in life comes easily, quickly, or cheaply. This particularly applies to the invaluable gift of a practical working knowledge of effective personal defense. Serious students, therefore, will want to invest some time, effort, and a bit of expense in setting up an area in which to work out and practice at home. This will be the place dedicated to your private practice of self-defense techniques, and your development as a martial artist. As much as possible, make it into a place you find peaceful and inviting, and where you will not be interrupted or disturbed during your workouts.

In good weather, outside spaces work fine and can be as simple as a clearing in a woods, park, or your backyard. Better yet, because it is available in any weather, is an indoor space, which might be a part of your living room or bedroom, or if you have more space, a spare bedroom or a garage or corner of a barn. The ideal, of course, is not always available; be creative and work with what you have. The space should have a clean floor, clear of all obstructions. Windows are important for lighting and ventilation. The best arrangement for the flooring will provide for some impact-absorbing material, such as high-density foam rubber and/or low-pile carpet (or canvas), so that you can practice falls and rolls without injury. This type of arrangement is usually referred to as the "mat." Obviously, you won't want to wear your street shoes on the mat area. Isolation from distracting noises is a good idea, both for you and for family members and neighbors who may not wish to be disturbed by stray sound from your practice. When my space was set up in a densely populated urban area, I took notices around to all of the immediate neighbors, informing them that any yelling they heard at my place was probably just me practicing my martial art, and not a situation requiring the police. The note invited anyone bothered by it to let me know, but no one ever did.

Aside from a qualified, live-in instructor, your best friend in your private training hall will be a mirror, preferably one large enough to permit a full head-to-toe view. This can be as simple as a narrow mirror mounted on a closet door, or as elaborate as a bank of floor-to-ceiling mirrors along each wall of the room. However elaborate or simple, your mirrors are important for checking your posture and techniques, and for evaluating the efficiency of your moves in transition between stances.

For many of the techniques we will be working with, it is very helpful—even necessary—to have at least one heavy bag ("punching bag") or a resistance target which you can build yourself at very little expense. An appendix at the back of this book provides advice on how to construct either a resistance target or an inexpensive bag with handy materials, but if you would like to purchase one ready-made, they are available in many sizes, weights, and coverings from specialty houses dealing in martial arts and sports training gear.

Hang the heavy bag (or your custom-made resistance target) securely so that it won't come down while you are practicing your sturdiest kicks and punches. The resistance targets are not as heavy as the bags but offer such realistic resistance to practice strikes that many people prefer them to the ready-made bags. The bag or target should be free to swing and sway without crashing into your walls or mirrors. Mount the bag so that the "strike zone" (middle portion of the target or bag) ranges from your head height to just below your hips.

The last item of training gear to consider is clothing. Some people prefer to get a uniform designed specifically for the purpose, such as a karate *gi* or taekwondo *dobok,* from a martial arts supply house. Lightweight cotton uniforms are a good way to start, and they are usually moderately priced. Some folks prefer a pair of shorts and a tank top or sports bra. Bruce Lee was known to work out in a simple pair of sweats and a Mickey Mouse tee-shirt. In a formal martial arts school you will want to wear the uniform worn by the other students. In your private workout space, you call the shots. The key is to get clothing that is comfortable, sturdy, roomy enough to allow very free movement, easy to clean frequently, and which you don't mind getting sweaty, dirty, and even ripped. A water bottle completes your ensemble, and you're good to go.

These few items are the only basics required for a fully functional home *dojang* and are all you'll need to make the best use of the programs presented in this book. As you progress with your study, you may elect to add other bags of different sizes and weights (for example, I use three: one full-length, a shorter one for torso shots, and a "head" bag).

Beyond these basic items, there is an ever-expanding range of equipment designed especially for martial arts enthusiasts. A variety of training gear specific to various styles has been developed over the years, and these items are becoming more widely available, such as the wooden dummy used in many Chinese systems, the *makiwara* familiar to Okinawan and Japanese *karateka,* and so on.

While you can always add extra "bells and whistles" at a later date, it is best (at least initially) to keep things simple, so that you can stay focused on what you're trying to accomplish rather than get caught up in the external trappings.

Remember that a student who diligently practices three or four times a week in a humble garage will learn more, faster, and better than the *dilettante* who dabbles once or twice a month at the most lavishly appointed country club.

This is *your* space, so fix it up to your liking. Questions of aesthetics are up to you. Traditionally, the décor in training spaces is very simple, even spare, the better to stay focused on the work. Some prefer a little incense or background music; others appreciate silence and an open window or door for fresh air. Traditionally, pictures on the walls, if any, are kept to a minimum. A bonsai might sit unobtrusively in a niche somewhere, but overall, the fewer distractions, the better.

One final consideration for those who are working in their own space is whether to practice solo or with a training partner (or several), and again, because this is your personal *dojang,* that's your call.

If you do elect to share this very special place, and your practice, with anyone else, be sure to stay well within your comfort zone. Be very choosy about who you admit, and make sure that they are people you can trust and with whom you are comfortable.

Be especially wary about inviting any self-proclaimed "experts" into your personal *dojang* space. If they're such hot shots, they should have their own school and students.

If they don't, there may be some very good reasons for that situation. If you want an expert, seek out a qualified instructor at a reputable school. That way, if things don't work out the way you expect, you can always walk, and you don't have to worry about unwelcome surprises turning up in your personal space, uninvited.

This is, after all, your private, personal *dojang,* and *you* decide who, if anyone, is welcome to enter and work out there with you.

KIHAP: THE POWER SHOUT

Sound is one of the fundamental universal energies—a good loud yell is the one primary act that most of us perform with our first breath. We arrive on the planet with two inbred fears—fear of falling and of loud, sudden noises. The fear of loud noises is instinctual, "hard-wired" into us at subconscious levels. This fear cannot be overcome by ordinary training or conditioning, which means that if you produce a loud enough yell suddenly enough, virtually everyone will react—usually in highly predictable ways.

Martial artists have been exploiting these predictable reactions for millennia. The physical force and mental (and emotional) power of a strong, sudden yell are easily observable. In practical, on-the-ground terms of effective self-defense, a good strong yell may be one of the most powerful weapons you can develop for your personal arsenal of unarmed-combat tools.

As with other aspects of martial arts training, these shouts have long been cultivated for very specific reasons. Called *kihap* ("kee-yop") in Korean, and *kiai* ("key-eye") in Japanese, the so-called "spirit yell," by whatever name, is regularly heard emanating from the training halls of martial arts schools the world over.

The power shout or *kihap* does not come from the throat or lungs, or even from the stomach, but is envisioned as emanating from *t'an t'ien,* the center of gravity in the human body (see the section on Centerline).

In real-life defensive combat, the predictable reactions to a well-developed *kihap* affect both you and your adversary. In your case, the effects are positive, including reinforcement—at both conscious and pre-conscious levels—that you are ready to fight, mobilizing adrenaline instantly to prime your body and sharply focus your mind for immediate action. In an actual self-defense situation, a sufficiently loud shout might even summon the curiosity and aid of passers-by.

Conversely, a powerful shout can demoralize, frighten, disorient, and even momentar-ily paralyze your attacker, who may "freeze" for the critical fraction of a second you need to launch a pre-emptive or responsive strike.

Beginning students frequently ask what their *kihap* should sound like. The answer is that it doesn't matter, because the *kihap* is unique to each individual. Short, sharp, single-syllable *kihaps* usually work best, although in some situations two or three, and in the case of multiple-technique combinations even more syllables may be employed.

Any sound will do; start with what comes naturally to you. The day will come when you are practicing a technique so intently that you will have forgotten entirely about shouting consciously, and you will be surprised suddenly to hear a natural, powerfully resonant shout spring spontaneously from your inner depths, ringing off the surrounding walls, trees, or mountains. That sound is *your* individual power shout.

WHOLE-BODY POWER

In the sections dealing with kinetic theory, we discussed aiming for the ideal of employing "total power" in the performance of defensive techniques. We also considered the "A.C.T." principle as a primary tool in developing total power. Another relevant and key concept in

Shindo is "whole-body power" or "full-body movement," which means pretty much what it sounds like: learning to involve the entire body in the performance of each technique. Again, as with most ideals, this is probably not perfectly achievable, but it makes a worthy target toward which to strive. If at first you can't integrate the movement of your entire body weight into a given technique, it may be that you can involve movement of perhaps half your total body weight, and more with practice over time. Let's examine some of the advantages.

It's time to create two imaginary characters for the sake of clear illustration of some of the theories. Since they're your imaginary characters, you can call them whatever you like; we will use "Attacker" and "Defender." Let's assume that Defender is a female, weighing 120 pounds, and that Attacker is a male, weighing 180 pounds. Let's further assign arbitrary percentages of body weight to various portions of their respective anatomies: 10%, say, to each of the arms, and 10% to the head; 20% to each leg, and the remaining 30% to the torso.

In that case, Attacker will have arms weighing 18 pounds apiece, each leg will weigh 36 pounds, his trunk 54 pounds, and his head 18 pounds, totaling 180 pounds. Our Defender will have arms weighing 12 pounds each, each leg will weigh 24 pounds, her torso 36 pounds, and her head 12 pounds, for a total of 120 pounds. Attacker outweighs Defender by 60

pounds, a considerable difference in size. How can Defender hope to defend herself against this much larger antagonist? Read on, and we shall see!

Let's consider a theoretical situation in which each attempts to punch the other. Initially, both are standing in a right natural fighting stance ("ready" stance—refer to the section on Stances). For now, let's just assume that each person has both feet planted firmly on the ground and is punching by moving the arm only. Recalling from our earlier discussion of kinetic theory that a foot-pound is equal to the force of one pound traveling the distance of one foot (in the direction of the force applied), we can begin to formulate some working theories concerning the relative power of their respective attacks (in this case, punches). Recognizing that we are here dealing with some very complex dynamics and equations, let us agree to forgo quibbles about some of the many obvious variables. Defender's arms, for instance, will not likely be quite as long as Attacker's, so that her punch will not travel exactly as far as his will.

Upon that agreement, let's assume that the punch of each, providing that they move *their arms only,* will travel two and a half feet. Each keeps their feet in place and neither twists the trunk; only the arms move. Under those theoretical conditions, let's see what happens when they punch. Being martial artists, and hence polite, we'll let Defender punch first. Defender's

12-pound arm and fist, traveling 2.5 feet, will deliver 30 foot-pounds *(f/p)* of force at the target (i.e., 12 lbs x 2.5'= 30 *f/p*). Ouch!

Okay, Attacker's turn. His 18-pound arm and fist, traveling the same 2.5-foot distance, will generate 45 *f/p* of force, or 50% greater force than Defender (Defender's 30 *f/p* + 50% [15] = 45 *f/p*). Double ouch! But now let's give Defender a quick course in martial arts self-defense and access to a little Shindo kinetic theory, and see what happens. Fast-forwarding three months into the future, let's award Defender a gold belt and give her another swipe at Attacker. This time, Defender keeps her feet static (as before), but with three months of practice under her new belt, she now twists her trunk to extend her reach another half-foot. Her punch now travels 3 feet instead of 2.5 feet.

Defender is still the same weight, so her arm and fist still weigh 12 pounds, which now travel 3 feet to her target and deliver 36 *f/p* of force [12 x 3 = 36]...but wait! It gets better. Because Defender has twisted her trunk (which, as we earlier determined, weighs 36 pounds) and has moved that weight a half-foot toward her target, Defender picks up another 18 *f/p* to add to the power of her punch. With this new, improved punch, Defender will deliver a total of 54 *f/p* of force (36 +18)—*more* than Attacker's original 45 *f/p* of force!

Attacker, of course, could make the same improvements to his technique and come up, under the same circumstances, with 81 *f/p* of force at his target—so Defender had better get out of the way.

(Getting out of the way, while we're on the subject, is a fundamental martial arts skill. See the sections on Centerline and Crescent Steps.) Defender, however, can relax a bit in the knowledge that it is not likely that a jerk like Attacker will, in most cases, study martial arts to any significant degree. The cowardly sort of bully who picks on smaller victims like Defender usually lacks the determination, perseverance, intelligence, or character required to pursue a demanding regimen such as martial arts study. Moreover, any legitimate martial arts instructor would unceremoniously toss such an individual out on his ear the moment such behavior became apparent. I have personally thrown at least three characters of that sort out of my classes over the years; people of that caliber use this knowledge with bad intentions and therefore are not worthy of being taught techniques such as these, relating to honor and awareness. Most martial artists are not only gentlemen and gentlewomen, but real men and women who would never stoop to misuse their knowledge, let alone dishonor their art, by abusing anyone. Defender need fear no such behavior from properly trained martial artists. Rather, she may confidently rely on any genuine martial artist in the vicinity to come unhesitatingly to her aid in time of need—in some cases, possibly even without her being aware of the intervention on her behalf.

But enough of Attacker; let's assume that he never learns discipline, never really grows up, and remains an untrained oaf all of his sorry days. Because Defender, however, perseveres in her training, she will be more than ready for any future encounters. Let's follow her development just a bit further. Aware of the principle of full-body movement, or whole-body power, Defender continues to practice and learns to shift her entire body weight, coordinating that movement into her punch. If, for example, without moving her feet, she simply "rocks" forward so that she shifts her body weight forward one foot, she would add a force of 120 pounds to her punch. In her last try, remember, she developed 54 *f/p* of force.

To this she now adds 120 pounds (her entire body weight moving a distance of one foot) for a total force of 174 *f/p* at the target—more than enough to ruin Attacker's day.

Granted, the above are theoretical ideals. In real life, with its myriad of variables, these figures will hardly be strictly accurate. Nonetheless, the underlying theoretical principles are sound, and by harnessing her entire body weight into whole-body movement and coordinating that movement into her technique, Defender will increase the potential power of her technique many times over.

Like our Defender, you can increase the power of your techniques using the same principles. All that is required is practice. Your heavy bag will be your best friend in developing your power in this way. Start by facing your bag flat-footed, and punch with your arm only. Notice how little the bag moves. Now twist your waist and add the weight of your torso (and increase your reach!). Compare the impact on the bag. Over time, add other elements as you become more familiar with and practice the many other practical techniques taught in this book.

Incorporate the A.C.T. principles. Drive power from your rear heel, through your *t'an t'ien,* coordinate your breathing, and project out *through* the target. Again compare the impact on the bag. Add "snap"—retracting your weapon quickly to the ready position. Learn to harness the power of your *ch'i,* utilizing your *kihap.* "Rock" forward, adding your entire body weight to the punch. Take a full step forward, adding distance as well. In each case, note the difference in impact. Hone what works for you, and discard what does not. Don't assume it will all come together immediately. Do expect to see slow—but definite—progress over the weeks and months and years as you continue. Don't get bored if you find yourself "stagnating" at a "plateau." Strive to make each performance just a bit better than the last.

Keep at it, and you will eventually be

rewarded with your next breakthrough. The best advice any experienced instructor can give you will be to persevere; don't give up. Remember that in the old fable, the race went to the tortoise, not to the hare. The real treasures of the martial arts—and of the serious study of self-defense techniques—do not reveal themselves casually. The insights of real value come only to those who stick with it for the long haul.

STANCES

Stances are postures, usually defensive, assumed by martial artists during the performance of their art, in practice, and when engaged in sparring or actual self-defense. While there are scores—even hundreds—of possible stances, the needs of basic self-defense will be adequately served with a solid command of four of the most versatile and commonly used positions.

Just as no two people are built exactly alike, so will there necessarily be some small variation in performance of these stances from one person to another. Taking individual variation into account, it is nevertheless advisable to incorporate all of the fundamental elements of each stance into your own version. To this end, beginners are best advised to follow the models provided as closely as possible—waiting for the experience of later years before developing personal modifications to customize each stance to individual preference.

The four basic stances we will examine, practice, and develop for inclusion in your personal toolbox are (with some variance in names or minor alterations in position) compatible with most systems or "styles" of martial art, worldwide. In our system, they are called the Fighting or "Natural Ready" Stance *(Seogi Chunbi)*, the Horse Stance *(Kiba Dachi)*, the Cat Stance *(Neko-Ashi Dachi)*, and the Conversational or "Casual" Stance.

Using the related pictures as guides, read through and then practice each of the four basic stances until they feel comfortable and natural to you, and you are able to move into them readily and quickly—at a moment's notice. Be sure that you feel solid and well-balanced (i.e.,

Horse Stance *(Kiba Dachi)*

Fighting Stance *(Seogi Chunbi)*

that you are maintaining a strong "root") in each stance.

Once you get to this level of confidence and competence in the stance, congratulations! You're ready to add it to the arsenal of defensive tools you're building in your toolbox. Remember the caveat about maintaining your tools, and be sure to keep them in good shape, sharp, and rust-free by pulling them out regularly (not just now and then) for practice.

The Horse Stance, above, is the stance into which we move on either of the commands "*Chun-bi*" (ready), or "*ku-mahn*" (stop), usually at the beginning and at the end of each exercise.

Head, shoulders and hips are squared to the front. Chin up, shoulders low, knees slightly bent, weight low in t'an t'ien.

The arms guard the ribs, elbows slightly bent, fists six inches in front of pelvis, palms in, thumbs facing each other about four inches apart. Feet are planted firmly, well wider than shoulders.

Dynamic muscular tension is maintained in all systems below the neck, including the feet, which "grip" the ground. All senses are keenly alert in all directions.

For the Fighting Stance, above, imagine standing on a giant clockface with 12:00 directly ahead. From the *kiba dachi*, or ready

Cat Stance *(Neko-Achi Dachi)*

"Casual" or "Conversational" Stance

stance, step back (usually with the right foot) into an "L" stance with the right foot pointing out to approximately 3:00, and the lead foot pointing straight ahead to 12:00.

Relax the shoulders and lower weight into t'an t'ien, flexing the knees for light mobility and quick movement. Chin up and back straight, remember to breathe deeply all the way to *t'an t'ien.*

Elbows guard ribs, and fists (lightly clenched) cover the face.

The gaze is broad, taking in the entire opponent and peripheral areas.

In Cat Stance, above, 90% of the weight is shifted onto the rear leg, leaving the front foot ready for a quick snap kick or *moo rop* —usually to knee, groin, or solar plexus (note lead foot withdrawn back toward rear leg).

Here, the practitioner has splayed her hands out into a *biu ji ("shooting fingers")* or tiger claw configuration in order to draw attention away from the preparatory withdrawal of her lead leg.

Cat stance can be used to good effect in tight quarters.

The final stance here is the Casual or Conversational Stance, shown above. Attacks are not always prefaced by obvious aggression; sometimes it may not be appropriate to adopt an overtly defensive posture at first. The "conversational" stance provides adequate—and inconspicuous—cover and readiness to respond instantly if need be.

Note that the feet take a "casual" half-step back into *seogi chunbi*, while the arms sub-tly cross to cover the chest—*lead arm on top*, allowing for quick lead-arm block, eagle wing to face, or other response, should need arise suddenly.

BASIC BLOCKS

Blocking techniques are employed to prevent, deflect, redirect, or minimize the effectiveness of an incoming blow, and they rely on the timely interposition of some object between the incoming weapon and the intended target—you. While external objects (a book, a chair, a baseball bat) can also work well in this application, blocks are usually effected using body weapons. While it is true that at advanced levels, special body weapons (feet, knees, etc.) may be employed, because this book deals with basic personal defense, we will here limit our examination to the most commonly used blocking weapons—the hands and forearms.

As we have discussed elsewhere in this book, a true martial artist would attempt as a first option to avoid altogether any situation that would result in a blow and, as a second option, to evade such a blow. The hard blocking techniques considered here would therefore come into play only as a last resort, when escape and evasion have failed, and immediate physical defense is an unavoidable necessity. Under those circumstances, blocks are ordinarily followed immediately by an unhesitating counter-attack

sufficient to conclude the confrontation. There are, however, some important exceptions to this caveat; refer to the chapter on "Situationally Appropriate Response."

Most martial arts systems and styles assign techniques to one or more of three general areas of the human body: high, middle, and low. The terminology and exact cut-off points may vary from one style to the next, but most styles regard the "low" zone as everything from approximately the level of the hips and below. The middle or "mid" zone is generally regarded as the region from the hips to the shoulders, and the "high" zone is usually considered to consist of the neck and head.

While there are literally scores of effective blocks against various strikes and attacks, we will focus on the four blocks likely to be most immediately accessible and reliably effective against the more common types of street attack. These four versatile basic blocks are the Low Block, Middle Block, High Block, and Stepping Cross, or "Closing Hammer" Block. Again, our operating premise is that while study of only a few techniques hardly constitutes a comprehensive knowledge of the martial arts, sound and effective basic self-defense does not require mastery of a great number of techniques. In an actual self-defense situation, one or two good techniques—or at most, three or four—should do the job.

Much more is involved in even the simplest low block than merely moving the arms and hands alone. All of the other factors considered thus far are particularly important for effective blocking technique.

Incorporation of all these elements (such as centerline, breaking the root, etc.) into even the seemingly simplest technique does initially require sustained concentration and considerable practice; but don't let the seeming complexity overwhelm you at first. Everything's tough when it's new. Don't forget how long it took to learn to ride a bike or drive a car! Remember that, in time, it will all come "automatically," as you learn to perform in a state of *mushin*. These techniques are not difficult—they merely demand a bit of practice—and there is no "magic" involved, just tenacity and determined perseverance.

As you practice each of the basic blocks, use your mirror to check for proper execution on each repetition. Are you using your whole-body power in each technique? Are you taking a quick crescent step off the line of attack as you ready and deliver each block? As soon as you begin to develop a little familiarity with each of the basic blocks, introduce a quick side step (see the sections on "Crescent Steps" and "Line of Attack") to quickly remove yourself to a position of at least momentary safety, and execute each block from this safer position to the side of your attacker. With practice, the side step and block will become virtually simultaneous. Are you staying loose until the moment of impact, tightening momentarily, and then loosening your hand and arm up again for a snappy return to ready stance? Be sure to keep your shoulders relaxed, elbows heavy—don't let tension creep up into your neck and shoulders, bringing your weight high again.

Every five or ten reps, shake out your shoulders and neck, and smile. You won't smile at a real attacker, of course, but it can help you learn to relax while practicing blocking drills. Keep your weight low in *t'an t'ien,* but remain light on your feet. Run ten reps with each arm in the air, using your mirror, then break briefly, shake out tension, and do another ten reps with each arm on your heavy bag. Don't forget to breathe powerfully out (power shout or tiger cough exhalation) and *through* your target with each technique.

LOW BLOCK

One of the four basic blocks taught in most martial arts, the low block covers the body from the hips down.

Most attacks to this area will, of course, be kicks, so it is worth investing the time and practice to learn to shift or crescent-step quickly to the side (off the line of attack) while executing this block in order to minimize the impact on your hand and arm.

Remember to breathe out strongly, and to drop your entire body weight into the block, bending your knees. Keep your back straight—do not lean into the block! Maintain high guard with the other hand.

MIDDLE BLOCK

The second basic block covers the torso from hips to shoulders. It is executed by simply turning the lead hand outward so that the palm faces outward. Block only to the edge of the body—there is no point in wasting time or energy covering empty space.

Be sure to breathe out powerfully from *t'an t'ien*, and rotate your entire body weight into the block from the back heel.

The *shuto* or knife-hand block shown in the illustration is used by some advanced practitioners, but beginners should stay with a side-fist hammer (closed-fist) block until they have acquired considerable experience with this technique. Maintain guard with your rear hand.

Low Block

Middle Block

HIGH BLOCK

The third basic block is the high block, which protects the head. Simply punch straight up to a position about three to four fist-widths in front of, and just above, the top of your forehead.

High Block

Crossing or Stepping Hammer Block

Even advanced practitioners usually use a side-hammer (closed-fist) block in this application. Note that the angle of the arm is like the roof of a house, so that blows will glance off, like rain running off a roof. Do not hold the forearm horizontally, as it can break with heavy impacts. Nor should you hold it too straight vertically, as that affords too little protection to the head. Work on developing the "house roof" angle.

As with all blocks, breathe out strongly from *t'an tien,* and remember that the punch is not with the arm only but initiates from the back or "anchor" heel.

CROSSING HAMMER BLOCK

The fourth basic block incorporates a preemptive step which slips inside the incoming strike to deliver a powerful closing cross-block with a side-fist hammer.

In the illustration, the Defender initially had her right foot forward, and she has stepped forward with the left foot while quickly bringing her left guard hand inward across the Attacker's centerline to strike the inside of his attacking forearm with a closed-fist hammer.

Be sure to breathe out strongly from *t'an t'ien,* and remember to keep hips and shoulders in a straight line—do not twist or turn at the waist.

Tip: An eagle wing back-fist to the nose (with the same hand) is a good follow-up from this block.

CRESCENT STEPS

One of the first—and most important—techniques we learn in Shindo is to get quickly off the line of any incoming attack.

One of the best ways to accomplish that objective is with a quick *crescent step* to the side.

In order to capitalize on the element of surprise, crescent steps are almost always taken very suddenly, and at the "last moment" before contact. If the step is taken too soon, the attacker is warned and may have time to correct the angle of attack in order to hit you despite your evasive action.

As its name implies, the crescent step is *curved,* like the crescent moon. Crescent steps can be large or small; a small crescent is usually thought of as being approximately equal to a quarter-circle, and a large crescent step is regarded as being roughly equivalent to a half-circle.

In the diagram below, **A** = the attacker, and **D** = the defender—you. The straight arrow is the attacker's intended line of attack, aimed (naturally) at the position you occupied when the attack was launched.

Almost always, crescent steps move first to either side—in order to get you quickly off the line of attack. However, because the crescent step is slightly *curved,* the step will also take you either forward or backward as well.

In any attack situation, it is helpful to mentally envision yourself and the attacker as standing on an imaginary circle on the ground. If you now imagine the circle as a giant clock face, assume that you are standing at the 6:00 position, and that the attacker is coming at you from the 12:00 position. Your quick crescent step moves you from your original position at 6:00 to the 3:00 position—i.e., 90° to your right.

You are now in a position of momentary safety, to A's side. Any responding counter-attack you make from this position will be much more effective because the attacker's force and focus are still moving along A's original line of attack, toward the place you were standing before your sudden crescent step.

Crescent Steps figure 1

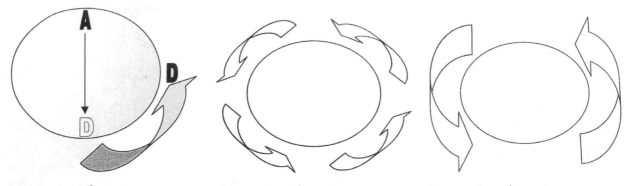

Crescent Steps figure 2   Crescent Steps figure 3   Crescent Steps figure 4

Practice moving in both opening and closing crescent steps around a circle on the floor, first moving "clockwise," i.e., stepping out with your left foot and quickly dragging the right foot behind to assume a solid "L" stance facing the center of the circle and looking toward 3:00 from the 9:00 position, then another, facing the 6:00 position from 12:00, and so on around the circle. Reverse direction and move in four small crescent steps around the circle "counter-clockwise."

Gradually increase speed and length of stride until you can smoothly and quickly step completely around the circle in just two large semi-circular crescents.

Keep your guard up and your stance solid as you complete each step. Move the lead (forward) foot quickly to your target position, then immediately drag the rear foot up into a place that puts you back in a solid "L" stance in your new position.

Stay loose and focused, weight low in *t'an t'ien* as you transition to each new position. Quick, easy, gliding footwork is one of the first and most important defensive skills you will learn in Shindo.

Lift the feet only as high as necessary to move quickly; try to maintain contact with the ground in a gliding or shuffling move rather than picking your feet entirely up off the ground. This helps keep your weight low and makes you more stable and less vulnerable to foot sweeps, trips, or other attempts to break your root as you move.

The more you practice this technique, the better you will get at it, eventually developing the ability to move very swiftly while maintaining solid footing and keeping your stance "closed," never taking your eyes off your attacker, and presenting no opening or opportunity for the attacker to breach your defenses as you move.

CARRY THE WATER

You have probably seen old movies or period illustrations of feudal times in which Chinese workers in the famous conical "coolie" hats labored to carry buckets of water suspended from poles carried across their shoulders.

Many did not realize that those poles were often tapered at the ends—the better to slip the buckets off and whip the poles into action as weapons in event of need.

The use of the poles as traditional weapons known as *bo* (or *bong*, in Korea) is, in fact, still practiced in some schools to this day.

In our schools of Shindo, we use this analogy to stress the importance of maintaining the hips and shoulders in a straight line as we move, rather than twisting or torquing at the waist.

Moving in this way seems a bit awkward at first, but the stability of stance and the solid footing referred to as a strong "root" that result from mastering this fundamental skill will more than justify the time and effort invested to acquire them.

Start out standing in a strong horse stance. Feel the stability of your stance and the strength of your "root." Now turn or twist at the waist.

Notice how your stance weakens, and your "root" becomes less stable. Twist far enough, and you'll fall over. Now try pivoting on one foot, while stepping around with the other, maintaining the line of hips and shoulders. Turn all you like, and still keep your strong, stable root.

Now move back into a strong horse stance and move one foot forward, bringing your entire body forward in the same stance, maintaining the straight line of hips and shoulders. At first this will seem heavy, awkward, and clumsy; but so was normal walking when you first started to learn that skill. Keep at it and you'll get better, faster, and lighter on your feet, without losing the power of the straight line of your hips and shoulders as you move.

When moving forward (or stepping back, to the side, or in circles), work to avoid twisting or torquing at the waist, hips, or knees. Instead, take the steps necessary to keep your hips and shoulders in a straight line. Any tradeoff in a sliver of speed will be more than compensated for by greatly increased stability and power.

One good way to reinforce this practice is to actually place a pole across your shoulders as you move. If you don't happen to have a *bo* handy, a broomstick or mop handle will do. This drill reinforces keeping your shoulders and hips in a straight line while moving. Once you begin to get the shoulders down, try holding the pole across your hips, and work with that for a bit (the buckets of water are optional!).

Again, this will feel cumbersome at first, but the payoff when you master the technique is well worth the effort.

As a helpful mental trick, visualize yourself as a stick figure as you practice moving properly in all directions, learning to Carry the Water.

Twisting Strike

Stepping Strike

Twisting Strike—side view

Stepping Strike—side view

NATURAL WEAPONS:
THE TOOLS YOU WERE BORN WITH

When working with a group of new students at one of our schools or seminars, we always like to throw out this question: "If you were attacked in the shower, how many weapons would you have?" Most people answer "none." Initial looks of surprised disbelief usually greet the right answer: if you "arm" yourself with the knowledge gained in proper self-defense training, the truth is that you have many weapons available to you at all times, in any situation—instantly.

It's not really a trick question, of course; it's just that for most of us, the word "weapon" usually brings to mind some sort of artificial implement intended to do bodily harm—a knife, a gun, a baseball bat, or whatever. Artificial weapons taught in legitimate schools of martial arts (ordinarily only at advanced levels of study) usually consist of traditional weapons such as staves, swords, and, in some systems, converted farming implements. Artificial weapons of any sort, however, are always secondary in importance to the primary weapons of the true martial artist—the hands, feet, elbows, knees, and many other natural body weapons with which we are born.

Natural weapons have a great many advantages over the artificial kind; they are considerably less likely to be taken from you by an attacker and then turned against you; you have much better and more flexible control over the exact location, type, and degree of damage to be inflicted with them; they do not jam, explode, misfire, or discharge unexpectedly; and you don't need to buy ammunition for them (or, for that matter, purchase them initially). Maintenance is low; you don't have to worry about tragic accidents involving the kids playing with them, or inadvertent injury to innocent bystanders; used strictly in self-defense, they are legal; and, most importantly and best of all, they are with you always, literally "at hand," ready for use instantly—anytime, anywhere. Beyond these advantages, learning to use your body as an efficient defensive armory gives you immediate command of many different kinds of weapons, enabling you to meet a much wider variety of self-defense situations. Finally, relying on yourself for personal safety rather than on some hazardous bit of hardware builds strength, skill, poise, and an honestly earned, realistic sense of personal confidence.

Conversely, artificial weapons offer none of these advantages, and in fact present a number of very serious—and even potentially deadly—disadvantages.

Real martial artists have no need for such contraptions, anyway—and certainly no use for the false "courage" or rented "power" with which artificial weapons beguile the frightened and emotionally insecure. Those who rely on such devices for "quick and easy" illusions of security only delude themselves, and in many cases actually leave themselves at much greater risk than they would be without them.

Sadder yet are the clueless losers who use such devices in feeble attempts to "impress" or bully others. Big stuff when swaggering about with their little toys, these fools are invariably revealed, when they are cornered without them, as the gutless wonders that they really are.

Despite the veneer of "dramatic" glamour with which Hollywood so often attempts to paint handguns, it is transparently obvious to anyone in the real world that their use requires no skill, no honor, no intelligence, and nothing even remotely approaching real courage. Far better to develop the true skill, honest valor, and legitimate confidence that comes with mastering techniques of personal defense using the noble weapons that nature provides.

In this section, we will examine a number of natural body weapons, learning how to form them properly.

Later, in the section dealing with Applications, we will examine some of the self-defense situations in which they can be most effectively employed.

Using the illustrations as models, check each weapon you form in your mirror. Then spend some time working with each body weapon on your heavy bag or resistance target, or with a partner and shield, as described in the section on Setting Up. Invest the time required in order to be able to access each weapon instantaneously, and practice applying them—with full-body power and proper breathing—from any and all angles and directions you find suitable for each weapon as it relates to your own height, weight, body type, and preferences. The familiarity gained from diligent practice in these basics will enable you to apply the techniques to full advantage. Do try to resist the temptation to rush ahead and learn everything in the advanced chapters before getting a good handle on the basics, however "boring" they may seem to grow. We always tell our students that if a technique or sequence seems boring, it's a sure indication that they don't understand it yet. Remember that the more you practice, the better you'll get, the more comfortable and natural the weapons you're practicing with will feel to you, and the more quickly and confidently you'll be able to access and utilize your weapon(s) of choice—in future practice sessions and, in the event of a worst-case scenario, in real-life defensive situations.

WARRIOR TALK

You've bought the book, put together your personal workout space—your private *dojang*—and made the commitment to yourself to follow through with mastering at least the basics of effective personal defense. Congratulations on coming this far! It's time to discuss a bit of specialized terminology we'll be working with as we start getting down to brass tacks. Here's a short list of terms we'll encounter frequently in coming pages:

A = Attacker—the "bad guys" in our illustrations

D = Defender, the good guys

L = Left

R = Right

target = Where you intend to apply your technique—it could be the "bad guy" generally, or a specific spot on his anatomy

t'an t'ien = the center of gravity in your body. You're already familiar with this important concept from earlier chapters.

technique = Any self-defense move (e.g. a block, strike, grab, escape, etc.)

application = Typical way in which a technique may be used

combination = A series of techniques in sequence

Writing about martial art self-defense moves is a bit like trying to describe a dance verbally; it can be difficult and inexact. Nevertheless, we'll use the descriptions below to approximate the movements:

Straight: Moving in a straight line away from your *t'an t'ien* and out through the target

Rising / Dropping: Just what it sounds like

Opening: Moving in an arc outward and away from your centerline (previously discussed), as in a backhand slap

Closing: Drawing in toward your centerline, as if pulling someone in toward you for a hug

Crossing (or Cross): Moving across your own and/or the opponent's centerline

Entering: Stepping closely in toward your opponent's centerline, often nearly or actually touching

Withdrawing (or retreating): Stepping back and away from your opponent

Front, Back, and Side: (all self-explanatory)

PALM HEEL

The palm heel is a versatile weapon that can be used very effectively on both hard and soft targets, with a high degree of safety for the practitioner. Many strikes one might consider performing with a standard forefist can be performed more effectively and more safely with the palm heel.

Proper formation of the palm heel is shown below. The heel of the palm is the striking weapon. The fingers and thumb are pulled back well out of harm's way at the moment of impact. *Ch'i* (Qi) energy can be very effectively projected out through the target with this weapon. It is also useful for blocks and converts quickly for use in counter-captures and traps.

Palm heel can be used effectively in many applications. Thrusting upward, primary targets are the chin (uppercut) and the nose. Thrusting straight forward, the sternum, solar plexus, and nose are good targets. Striking from the side, the temple and ribs are vulnerable, and it is very effective against locked joints, especially the elbow. The palm heel is also very effective in dropping "axe" strikes, particularly to the bridge of the nose and clavicles (collar bones).

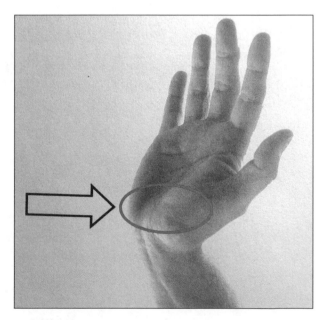

Palm Heel

Typical Applications—PALM HEEL

Up to jaw

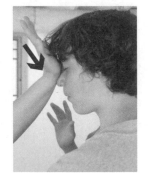

Down to bridge
of nose

Straight to sternum / solar plexus

Typical Combinations—PALM HEEL

D blocks attempted R punch
with opening L hammer
block . . .

. . . follows with same-hand
straight palm heel to nose . . .

. . . and finishes with R straight
palm heel to solar plexus.

SHUTO—THE SWORD HAND

Shuto ("sword hand") is the Japanese name used to describe the hand weapon most commonly associated with the so-called "karate chop" made famous in movies and popular entertainment on television. The striking surface is the fleshy pad at the little-finger side of the palm.

Primary targets with an opening *shuto* are the neck, philtrum, bridge of the nose, and, driving backward or to the side and down, the groin. On rare occasions, a closing *shuto* is used, with the palm facing up, to the temple or neck.

This weapon makes an excellent blocking tool, often preceded by a quick evasive step to the side (see "Crescent Steps"). The particular advantage of this weapon in blocking applications lies in the fact that, because the hand is already open, it can be wrapped around the attacking arm in a lightning-quick counter-capture, nearly simultaneously with the block.

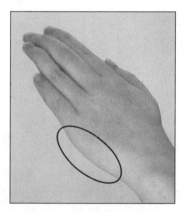

Sword Hand

Typical Applications—SWORD HAND

To throat

To groin

Closing Block

57

Typical Combinations—SWORD HAND

D foils attempted stab with crescent step to side and opening *shuto* block . . .

Block detail

. . . and immediately captures A's attacking wrist with the same hand, . . .

. . . pulling A off-balance, raising his arm to deliver a kick to the ribs, with further follow-up as required. At the moment in which A's attention is diverted by the kick, he will offer no resistance as D takes the knife. The same defense will work as well for a punch, grab, or shove.

SIDE FIST HAMMER / FOREFIST

Although used in entirely different ways, the side fist hammer and the forefist are formed identically, as shown below. Beginning with the fingers in a straight "salute" position, fold all four fingers down to touch the soft pads at the base of the fingers, then roll the folded fingers more deeply into the palm, cinching them in place with the thumb locked tightly across the middle knuckles of the first two fingers. When this weapon is used as a forefist, it is important to keep the wrist straight so that it does not bend or flex on impact. Because the small finger bones (phalanges) can be relatively eas-

ily damaged when used in forefist punches, we do not recommend use of the forefist except in rare circumstances, and then only against soft targets, such as the solar plexus.

The side fist hammer is a much more versatile tool, both more effective and safer for the practitioner. Used for blocks and for strikes, it may be deployed against a much wider variety of targets, including hard and bony areas. Principal targets are the temple, face, solar plexus, and ribs (in an opening arc from the side); the nose, clavicles, or sternum (striking downward); and the groin (downward and to the side or rear).

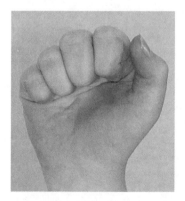

Fold fingers down

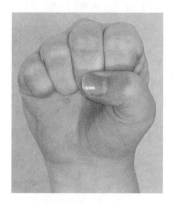

Lock them in place with the thumb

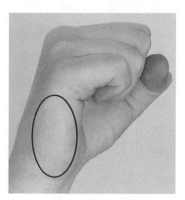

. . . and viola! You have a solid side fist hammer.

Typical Applications—SIDE FIST HAMMER

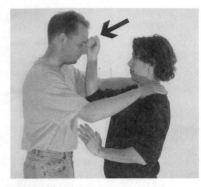

Striking down to nose

Down to side or rear, striking to groin

Striking down to clavicle

Typical Combinations—SIDE FIST HAMMER

A grabs D's hair.

Pinning A's hand to her head to minimize hair pull, D chambers side hammer . . .

. . . and steps back into A with hammer to solar plexus. Keep in mind that having a variety of self-defense tools allows for flexible responses to a wide variety of situations. The last strike could just as easily have been to A's nose, jaw, groin, or ribs, at D's option.

BIU JI—SHOOTING FINGERS

Biu Ji, the "Shooting Fingers" familiar to practitioners of Wing Chun and other Chinese styles, are straight finger jabs, usually to the face. *Biu ji* can be used as a distraction, invoking the startle response to break an attacker's concentration and balance, or, with full contact and greater force, as a jabbing penetration weapon to small target areas, especially the eyes and face.

Proper formation of *biu ji* is shown below. The fingertips comprise the weapon. *Biu ji* is delivered in either of two ways, depending on the intended effect. As a distraction, the motion is very quick and whip-like, involving only light contact with the target, if any. This application does not require body power; only the lightning-fast flick of the hand and arm are used, best accompanied with a sharp exhalation and a *kihap* (yell). Distractions of this sort are usually followed immediately with another attack using a more powerful, full-contact weapon (palm heel, knee or elbow strike, and the like).

When *biu ji* is used as a contact weapon, different body mechanics are employed. Instead of a quickly retracted whip-like motion, the fingers and palm of the hand are shoved past the face on a trajectory that extends beyond the target, driving the fingers and palm of the hand into the attacker's nose or chin, and pushing his head over backward. A full step forward is helpful in generating whole-body power.

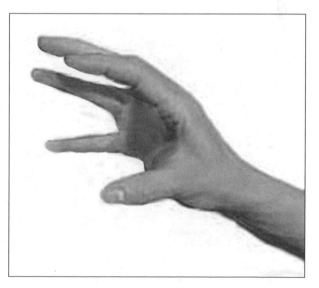

Biu ji

Typical Application—*BIU JI*

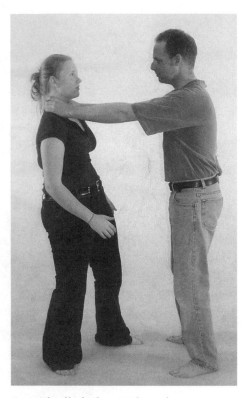

As with all chokes, D breathes
out to remain calm and decides
on an initial *biu ji* response.

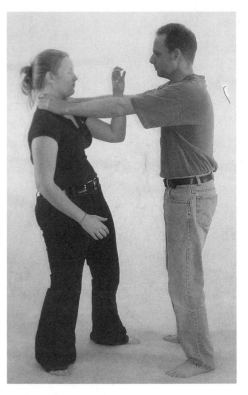

Sinking her weight to *t'an tien*
for stability, D raises her hand
up between A's arms . . .

. . . and strikes to A's face, breaking his hold,
concentration, and balance, and setting him up
for her next move.

Typical Combination—*BIU JI*

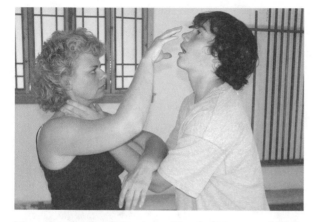

Trapping both of A's arms, D administers a *biu ji* strike to his eyes, . . .

. . . steps forward immediately with a palm heel blow to his chin, . . .

. . . and concludes with a knee to the groin.

EAGLE WING

The Eagle Wing is a refinement peculiar to Tao-Zen Ryu Shindo, reminiscent of the hand weapon anciently known in many Chinese systems as the "Ox Jaw," and it is used in many of the same ways. Eagle Wing differs from the classic Ox Jaw, however, in that the fingertips are not drawn together but are splayed stiffly (though narrowly) apart, and rigidly extended as though trying to touch the underside of the wrist.

The striking weapon is comprised of the ends of the radius and ulna, the long bones of the forearm, indicated by the circle shown in solid line.

More powerful and versatile than the standard backfist, and safer for the practitioner to use, eagle wing is employed in front rising strikes to the chin and groin; in opening front vertical arcs to face, clavicles, or sternum; obliquely and horizontally to the ribs and torso from the side; backward over the shoulder to the face; and to the groin in descending arcs to the side or rear. Eagle wing is also sometimes used as a block, and occasionally as an effective short-term dragging hook for transitional counter-captures (using the area indicated by the circle in dotted line).

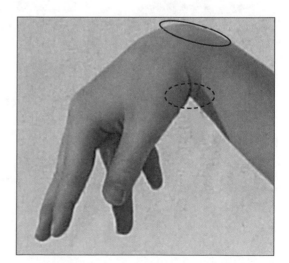

Eagle wing

Typical Applications—EAGLE WING

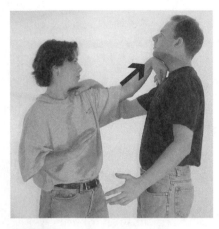

Up to jaw

Rising to groin

Back over shoulder to face

NOTE: Large arrows are intended to emphasize that power comes not just from the arms, but from the heels, using *whole-body power.*

Typical Combination—EAGLE WING

D blocks attempted R punch with closing L *shuto* block. (Note that D has prudently taken a quick crescent step out of harm's way.)

D follows the *shuto* block immediately with a same-hand eagle wing to the nose . . .

. . . and finishes with a R side kick to the solar plexus.

EMPI—ELBOW WEAPONS

Empi is the term used in Japanese martial arts for techniques using the elbow. Devastatingly effective at close range, the elbows may be used in both opening and closing arcs, moving back or forward, and on any plane: horizontal, vertical, or oblique.

Particularly useful in escapes, the elbow can be a good choice for an initial response when the defender is grabbed and held closely from the side or behind. Rarely used alone, elbow strikes are almost always employed in combination with other techniques.

There is no right or wrong way to form the elbow weapon; it pretty much is what it is. Pull your fist up close to your shoulder for vertical blows, and close to your sternum for horizontal strikes. Keep your upper arm close to your ribs until you actually strike, and then return it again to cover your ribs (i.e., return to a proper ready stance) immediately following each technique. It can be helpful on strikes to the side or rear to reinforce the *empi* (striking) arm by covering the fist on the striking arm with the free hand and using the power of both arms (and, of course, whole-body power) in the technique. As with all strikes, remember to breathe out forcefully on impact.

Because elbow techniques move a very short distance, they rely greatly on reinforcing whole-body movement for power. They are most effective when it is possible to take a full step when delivering the strike, in order to put as much weight and movement as possible behind the blow.

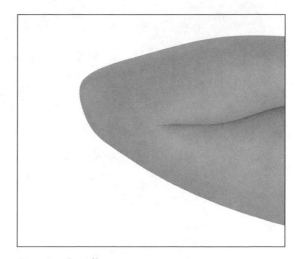

Empi—the elbow weapon

Typical Applications

Up to jaw

Horizontally to jaw

Back to solar plexus

Typical Combination

A attacks with half-nelson choke from rear.

D steps back into A with rear *empi* strike . . .

. . . and follows up with a rising rear eagle wing to the nose.

KICKS

FRONT ("SNAP") KICK

This is the fastest and most commonly used kick, especially by untrained fighters. Primary targets are the ankle, shin, knee, groin, and sometimes the solar plexus. While kicks to higher targets are possible with practice, they are ill-advised in street defense situations, for several reasons. Relatively unstable, kicks above the waist are slower to deliver, and slower in recovery (i.e., return to ready stance), and they offer far greater danger of interception and counter-capture by the attacker. While high kicks are quite showy and can be fine for flexibility and stretching or for tournaments and demonstration "forms" practice, in real-life defense situations, it is best to avoid kicks higher than the waist altogether.

The front or "snap" kick is initiated by drawing the knee of the kicking leg up toward the chest as quickly as possible. This movement is also called "cocking" or "chambering" the leg or kick. The foreleg is then whipped out and back with a very quick motion, as if snapping a towel or flicking water off the leg (as when emerging from a pool). The weapon is usually the ball of the foot, with care taken to pull the toes up and back out of harm's way on impact.

When practicing complex movements like kicks, it is helpful in the learning stages to break the move down into shorter segments, or "counts." Initially, practice the chamber (pulling the leg back up to the chest) as the "one-count," snapping the foot out through the target and retracting it quickly as the "two-count," and the step back down into a solid ready stance as the "three-count." Never with any technique, and especially with kicks, extend your arm or leg completely, even at full extension of your technique. Always keep it slightly bent as a protection against accidental hyperextension. As you gain greater experience with and confidence in your technique, begin coordinating all counts into one smooth, easy, quick process, and incorporate all other elements of good defensive technique, such as global awareness, mental focus, kicking *through* rather than just *to* the target, and proper breathing. Always return to a strong, centered ready stance, weight low, prepared to glide quickly and effortlessly into any follow-up techniques as may be required.

Be sure when practicing any technique, and especially kicks, never to start at full speed or power while your muscles are cold. Warm up thoroughly first with breathing and stretching exercises, and then perform the kick ten times at very slow speed and with perfect form, using each leg, then advance to moderate speed for ten reps with each leg, still with perfect form. Now you're ready to work on speed, remembering not to sacrifice balance. power, focus, or form. Be sure to return to proper fighting stance between each kick.

Remember with each practice session to incorporate proper breathing, keeping your weight low in *t'an t'ien*, projecting *qi* not just *to* but *through* the target, and recall that power comes not just from the kicking leg but from the rear or supporting heel, bringing whole-body power into the technique. Don't neglect your *kihap* (power shout) at the moment of full extension and penetration. Practice your kicks both in air for form, and with your heavy bag to get a feel for actual resistance. Start with light contact and work up gradually to heavier impacts. Build speed and power slowly, over time. Give it your best; don't cheat yourself with sloppy practice. You want the best self-defense tools you can build.

SIDE KICK

The side kick is useful at slightly longer range than the front snap kick. Though somewhat slower than the front kick, the side kick compensates with superior power, derived from a strong thrust from the hips. Primary targets are the ankle, knee, groin, or solar plexus. Side kicks may be launched while stepping in towards an attacker, while retreating, and from a stationary position. The weapon is the soft pad at the outside edge of the sole of the foot between the heel and the little toe, often called the *shuto,* or sword foot.

To execute a side kick, pivot on the ball of the supporting foot, twisting the hips and shoulders so that your body turns sideways-on to the target. As you turn, lean your head and torso down and away from the target, simultaneously drawing your kicking knee up to your chest, just as you would in chambering a front kick. Use your arms to cover, as always. The further you lean your head down, the higher your kick can be, but keep in mind that in real life, kicks are best kept below waist level.

With a bit of practice, the turn, lean, and chambering are all done in one smooth motion and can be regarded as the "one-count" during practice. Look over your shoulder at the target, and aim the heel and sole of the kicking foot directly on point. The "two-count" consists of sharply thrusting the leg straight out so that the sole, sword edge, and if possible, the outer edge of the heel of the kicking foot all penetrate the target, using a powerful hip thrust to drive the kick deeply through. Complete the "two-count" by sharply retracting the kicking leg to the chambered position, pulled tightly back to your chest. The "three-count" is completed by pivoting back around to face the target, and leaning upright as you stand back down into a strongly rooted ready stance. The pivot, lean, delivery, and recovery in this kick are fairly complex and require a good bit of practice to master, but the tool is handy enough to warrant the effort required.

BACK KICK

Back kicks share some similarities with side kicks, but instead of turning sideways-on to the target, your back is turned fully to the attacker, and the kick is directed behind you. The weapon

is the sole of the heel. This kick is handy in a variety of commonly encountered attack situations. Examples include attacks from the rear; situations in which you are attempting to escape a rear hold of some sort; and when dealing with multiple attackers from all directions.

Primary targets are the arch of the foot, ankle, knee, groin, and solar plexus. The familiar "stomp" and "crushing" steps are often regarded as variations of side or back kicks. The further you lean your head down, the higher you can get your kicks up. That's fine for stretching and practice drills, and it's good exercise. Just bear in mind that in real life, your best advice is to keep all kicks waist-high or lower.

As with the side kick, most back kicks begin by chambering the kicking leg, drawing it up toward your chest as you lean down forward, and quickly glancing back over your shoulder to ascertain the attacker's position with your peripheral vision.

Use this as the "one-count" for your practice drills. Immediately throw the back kick, straightening your leg to propel your heel through the target, and quickly retract to the chambered position as your "two count." The "three-count," of course, is your return to an upright, covered, and firmly rooted ready stance, facing your attacker, who will now have a good deal less starch in his sails.

COBRA KICK

The cobra kick is very useful at close quarters, in forestalling a rush, and in powerfully pushing an attacker away. Often employed in specialized types of attacks to the knee, it can be used for mild admonishments, simple takedowns, or to make more forceful points without serious injury to the recipient. In circumstances requiring stronger measures, it can very easily break a leg.

The cobra kick begins with the same sort of chambering used in the front kick. The cobra kick, however, differs from all other types of kicks in that the defender's foot is planted on the target area before the kicking leg is extended. Thus the cobra is really a pushing and shoving kick. The same technique performed with the hand or other portion of the defender's anatomy is sometimes referred to as a cobra shove.

The weapon is usually the sole, side, or ball of the foot. In practice, the "one-count" consists of chambering the kick and placing the foot on the target—physically, if using resistance equipment (e.g. a heavy bag, medicine ball, or the like), or by mentally locating an imaginary target if working in air. The "two-count" is comprised of a shove out with the kicking leg, using the degree of force appropriate to the situation envisioned. Unless kicking behind the knee, retraction to the chambered position may be more leisurely than with other kicks. Stand down to ready stance for the "three-count."

MOO-ROP: KNEE WEAPONS

Ask one hundred women what defensive tactic they think of first in close-range self-defense encounters, and you're virtually guaranteed to hear just about one hundred variations of the classic knee-to-groin strike. This old chestnut has been passed down from mother to daughter ever since Eve. If it works, the tactic can be spectacularly effective. If.

The downside, naturally, is that if you ask one hundred oafs what defense they would be most on guard against if attempting to visit unwanted attentions on a woman, you will unfailingly get another hundred versions of precisely the same answer. This is one of several reasons why, while everyone has heard the theory—and perhaps even used the technique jokingly or in horseplay—its successful use as an initial response in actual self-defense is very rarely seen. Don't dismiss the knee as an effective defensive tool just yet, however, for there are other, less anticipated, and more effective options with this powerful close-range leg weapon.

Unlike the other body weapons, the knee is quick and easy to learn. Chamber your leg; it's done. The trick is in how and where it is deployed. Since your would-be attacker is up close anyway, consider giving him a big old hug—and using the resulting stability to swing your entire body weight behind your knee and into his solar plexus, thigh, or just above his knee. The knee weapon is a great follow-up after, say, a kick or other strike that gets your assailant to bend forward. Knees work great for nose smashes if you can get the attacker's head low. And finally, that classic groin shot

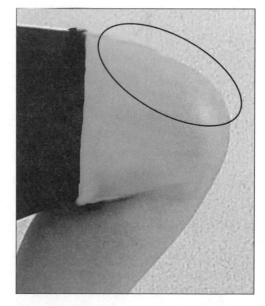

Moo-Rop Knee

that usually won't work as an initial tactic because it is anticipated can work wonderfully as a follow-up technique if you are able to distract your assailant and compromise his balance just long enough to give you an opening that is not guarded.

THE INFAMOUS HEAD BUTT

There are scores of possible body weapons, and probably hundreds of different techniques that could potentially be used in defensive situations. A listing of all the possibilities could fill a small library. Because this book deals with the *fundamentals* of self-defense, we have focused here on some of the most versatile, effective, and *basic* body weapons and defensive tactics. One in particular that is really in a category all its own has passed, with varying shades of authenticity, into popular folklore.

The infamous *head butt* is enjoying quite a vogue in the vulgar entertainments of the day. This is one "Hollywood technique" that actually can work very effectively in some situations, such as some types of chokes, and it is especially useful when locked in a "bear hug" (from in front or behind), with your arms pinned tightly to your sides. It is important to be aware that there is very definitely a right way—and a wrong way—to perform this technique. Done improperly, it can cause more damage to the person performing it than to the intended recipient. In a pinch, however, the head butt is a defensive tool of sufficient value

to warrant taking the time and trouble to learn how to use it properly.

Many see this technique in "chop socky" adventure films and assume that the heroine/ hero simply nods her/his head sharply forward (or back, if the attacker is behind), whacking the villain in the nose, and then flies/rides/transports off to save the town/ world/universe. While the nose-whacking part is correct, the mechanics of delivery, not so obvious on film, are important to the safety of any defender using this technique in real life. Most head butts are delivered to attackers holding the defender from the front. Typically, the arms are pinned tightly to the sides, and the bear hug is sufficiently close to preclude defensive use of the legs. In this circumstance, the head butt may be the only effective weapon available.

Those properly trained in the use of this technique incorporate the following four elements of correct performance:

1. Take a deep breath in, and *move your tongue* safely out of harm's way. Bring your teeth together, pushing your tongue firmly up against the hard palate just behind your

top incisors (front teeth). This protects against biting your own tongue accidentally on impact.

2. As best you are able, given the constraint imposed by the bear hug, square your shoulders and stand as nearly erect as you can in preparation for the strike.

3. Most students are surprised to learn this seemingly counter-intuitive but critically important caveat: *never nod or rock your head* (either forward or backward), *and do not in any way flex or bend your neck* when delivering head butts. While the head is the weapon that delivers the strike, the technique is driven *not* from the head, neck, or shoulders, or even from the waist (except in special cases, as when children are lifted entirely off the ground*), but *from the anchor foot*. The importance of maintaining a *straight line* from your feet up through your legs, back, neck, and head cannot be overemphasized. This is what ensures that your whole-body weight, and not just your head, powers the strike.

4. As with all strikes, remember to breathe sharply *out* on impact. If the head-butt technique is to the front, remember to *close your eyes* at the moment of impact. Noses in this situation can bleed profusely and with surprising speed; in the age of AIDS, caution is well advised.

Be sure that your striking weapon is the top of your forehead, not the bridge of your own nose—especially if you are wearing glasses. If your strike is to the rear, of course, the weapon is the top of the back of your head. Don't raise your chin or bend your neck to fling your head back; maintain a straight line from your heels to the back of your head, and strike with your whole body as a unit.

The bear hug is often seen in horseplay, where serious harm is not intended. Use your judgment to decide how much force is required in your response. What are the circumstances? Is this someone you know, who may be overstepping bounds, but in safe surroundings, with trusted others present? Where exactly are your hands pinned? Close enough to make an admonishing grab to the groin? In horseplay, that will often suffice to effect an escape, or you might try a gentler bump to the nose, instead of a full-on nose smash. It doesn't take much to break a nose, and very little to cause sufficient pain to secure immediate compliance with your demand for release. If, on the other hand, the assailant is a stranger in an alley obvi-

---

*Obviously, in the very rare case when a defender's feet are lifted off the ground, it will be necessary to flex from the waist and use the straight-line power of the upper body for the strike.

ously bent on real harm, a full-power response may be needed.

If you believe the situation is serious enough to warrant full use of the head-butt technique, it may also justify a quick spit into the attacker's face in order to provoke the startle response, breaking his root and concentration in order to set up your strike.

Be prepared for your attacker to stumble a step or two backward as he relinquishes his hold on you, and be ready to take a strong step for-ward to catch your own balance as he lets you go. Open your hands up and out to ward off the attacker's hands as he reaches in shock to grab his own face. Your forward step, of course, will land you in a strong stance for a follow-up kick or other technique as required.

Note in both front and rear head butts that D maintains a straight line from her heels to the striking point, and does not bend or flex her neck or raise or lower her chin. The strike delivers whole-body power behind the blow.

**Front Head Butt
preparatory**

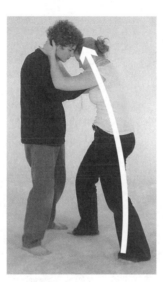
Front Head Butt

Rear Head Butt

DROPS:
THROWS, SWEEPS, AND TAKE-DOWNS

The Shindo syllabus of sweeps, throws, and take-downs is distinct from the "hard" techniques of this class usually found in other styles of martial art, in that the techniques of Shindo are generally more smoothly flowing and easier to execute, requiring much less force. In short, they are designed (as are all techniques in the Shindo syllabus) to work effectively for smaller and lighter practitioners.

There are many methods for taking an attacker to the ground, variously called "drops," "throws," "sweeps," or more generically, "take-downs," depending on how they are executed.

A drop can be made in any direction, but most are either to the front or rear. Many front throws in other martial arts systems involve grappling or wrestling with the opponent, and then "muscling" and *lifting* him up and over a hip or shoulder. This can work when size and/or muscle power is roughly equivalent, but the lifting element renders these techniques ineffective when the attacker is much larger or stronger than the defender.

Shindo throws, however, rather than attempting to lift an attacker, simply destroy his root (balance) and then pull and twist to guide him around the outer perimeter of the defender's stance.

Rear throws in most systems, including Shindo, seldom involve direct lifting, relying instead on leg trips and/or hip throws, or on leveraging the attacker's arms up and backward over his shoulders. While some of the more advanced rear throws of Shindo are somewhat more elaborate to learn, even the basic throws covered in this volume are highly effective, regardless of size or strength.

Reaping is a term used in many older martial systems to describe the swinging or "threshing" motion of the defender's leg when employed to sweep or kick an attacker's leg(s) out from under him. In Shindo, this motion is modified from a "swinging" motion to a deliberately solid planting of the "reaping" leg in the desired position. From this strongly rooted stance, the defender uses a "pulling" motion to roll power up from the ground in a smooth, continuous action through the toes, heel, calf, back of knee, thigh, and hip, pulling the attacker around with the shoulders and hips. This effectively "twists" or "coils" the energy up from the ground and along the defender's body in a wave-like fashion, destroying the attacker's root and guiding him inexorably around the outer perimeter of the defender's stance, and thence to the ground. With practice, the entire complicated-sounding sequence occurs in literally fractions of a second.

FORWARD/FRONT DROP

In the illustrations shown, the attacker (A) has attempted a punch or grab with her right hand, which the defender (D) has blocked and counter-trapped at A's elbow. D then uses her left elbow on A's right shoulder to drive A down and forward, pulling A off balance, destroying A's root. Continuing to pull A forward and down, D reinforces the arm capture with her other hand and pulls A's ribs and armpit strongly into D's hip. D then steps forward, turning her hips to the front to pull A further down, forward, across the front of D's body, and around the outside perimeter of D's firmly rooted stance, dropping A to the ground. Note that D's hips and shoulders are in a straight line as she finishes the throw. Note also that D retains hold of A's hand for control, to assist with her own balance, and to facilitate any further follow-up (kicks, etc.) as may be required, until the conflict is resolved to D's satisfaction.

Because the method used in Shindo takedowns eliminates the need for muscle power required to lift the attacker's weight off the ground, these throws work very effectively for smaller and lighter defenders.

Front Drop 1   Front Drop 2   Front Drop 3

Note in the illustrations that the defender moves her feet as required to keep her hips and shoulders in a straight line as much as possible, rather than twisting or torquing at the waist, as we learned in the section on "Carry the Water."

REAR DROP

Now let's take a look at how a Shindo roll-out is used to drop an attacker over backward. Dealing with an unwelcome side grab (1), the defender prevents the attacker from walking out of the drop by stepping behind his foot (2). Because the attacker now cannot step back without tripping, the throw is ensured. The defender opens her arm up and outward across the attacker's upper body and face (3), causing him to fall backward (4). In Shindo, this technique is called "Viewing the Milky Way."

Note that in any throw, the attacker will try whatever it takes to avoid falling, including grabbing on to you. This is why it is important not to bend at the waist as you drop the attacker; he could drag you down with him. Instead, keep your back straight, bend only at the knees, and sink into a very solid horse stance (5).

III. APPLICATIONS

APPLICATIONS:
DEFENSIVE RESPONSES

In the preceding section, we learned how to work with individual self-defense tools and techniques. Now it's time to begin putting some of them together into effective responses to common attack scenarios. Real-life attacks, of course, rarely mirror textbook examples exactly, but then, that's what *mushin* is for—to allow effective, spontaneously flexible responses to all kinds of assault situations. While no two assaults are ever identical, it is also true that attacks tend to fall into a few classic types and categories with amazing reliability. Virtually all attacks are attempted in highly predictable ways, and this consistency works strongly in favor of the aware defender.

To those who diligently practice the "reading" skills we discussed earlier, would-be attackers become an open book, "telegraphing" advance notice of their intentions through the body language of facial expression and physical movement. This is where the old Chinese adage, *"When the attacker moves, the defender is already in motion to meet him,"* comes into play. Your ability to read an attacker's body language accurately allows you to "scope out" the attacker's intentions, alerting you ahead of time to any incoming attempt. This knowledge enables you to predict with a high degree of accuracy how the attack will unfold—a very powerful advantage.

You have already given yourself another crucial advantage by investing the time, discipline, and effort required to put together a mental toolbox, stocking it with a broad variety of highly effective defenses, and learning from extensive practice how to use them appropriately.

In this section, we'll apply all of the above advantages to a variety of common attack scenarios. Keep in mind that your response to each scenario has many possible variations; if a strike to, say, a jaw is shown, you might just as easily elect to deliver a strike to a collarbone or the nose, or if the attack was sufficiently rude, perhaps to all three. *You* decide how to apply your tools; your options are endless.

While every physical attack will vary a bit in the details, they all share the same basic attributes:

- Every **conflict** consists of two basic elements, *attack* and *response* (i.e., defense).

☙ Every *attack* consists of one (or more) of three basic types of assault: *strikes* (punches and kicks); *captures* (grabs and holds); and *groundwork* (grappling).

☙ Every effective *response* consists of one or both of two basic defenses, *evasion and escape,* or, if required, a *counter-attack* sufficient to conclude the confrontation.

As you work with the defensive combinations in the Applications section, remember that self-defense techniques are best learned in much the same way that we practice scales on a musical instrument. Start slowly, with great attention to correct positioning and precise execution in each detail. Only after many repetitions do we begin to build speed and smooth performance, always retaining control of accuracy, focus, and power. Like most of the best things in life, good technique cannot be hurried. Really worthwhile skill develops only with much practice, over no little time. As Grandmaster Yun always admonished his students, *"Make haste slowly."*

Keep in mind all the elements of correct technique, including those that aren't so immediately obvious: breathing, whole-body movement, proper stance, energy centered in *t'an t'ien,* global awareness in all directions, and so on. If at first it all seems a bit much to coordinate, persevere. Remember that over time, just like learning to ride a bike, the day will come

when you no longer need to focus on the pedals and handlebars but can slip into a state of *mushin,* incorporating all elements into correct, effective performance, almost effortlessly. On that day, that technique becomes yours. Toss it confidently into your toolbox; no one can ever take it from you. Take care not to let it get rusty from lack of practice, and it will always be there for you, instantly, if ever you should need it.

Test your progress in your mirrors, on your heavy bag, and with your training partner(s). Every day and every hour that you practice strengthens your command of effective self-defense. Such knowledge is power indeed, and with it comes concomitant responsibility to use it only when all other options (including turning and walking away) have failed—and then *only* to the extent *absolutely necessary* to conclude the conflict. Read it again: *only* to the extent *absolutely necessary* to conclude the confrontation. Period. Not one jot more, however tempting it may be.

Whenever you determine that a given technique (or combination) is in fact *necessary* for legitimate self-defense (and such determinations are made in the blink of an eye), *go for it.* Once the decision is made, the time for hesitation or second thoughts has passed. Move instantly, with the full power and authority required to handle the job.

Each of the attack scenarios (and the corresponding defenses) presented in the Applications section will involve techniques that fall into one or more of the following general categories:

- strikes
- grabs
- groundwork
- weapons

As you work through the scenarios presented in this section, keep in mind that assault situations do not always fall neatly into just one type or another, and many may include elements of attack from two, three, or all four of the basic classifications we use in this book. No problem; we work with a wide variety of tools and tactics precisely in order to be prepared to deal with any of the common assaults you are likely to encounter.

Skim through the book once and set it on the shelf to gather dust, and you may not be ready if something untoward does arise. Use it as a resource to inform and guide regular practice, and you will be ready for whatever might come up. How ready do you want to be? How much are you prepared to practice?

Earlier in the book, we discussed setting up your private practice space—your personal *dojang*—and we talked about the advantages of having a trusted partner (or several) to work out with. In this section, the time has come to put the theory you've studied and the tools

you've developed to practical use. Kiss the couch goodbye.

Work carefully so as not to injure your partner (and vice versa!). Start slowly and gently, and build speed and power over time. Lots of time. Begin with very light contact and work into more realistic force very gradually, as your experience and tolerance for contact (and that of your training partners) and your mutual trust increase. Develop a clear system of communication that includes commands you both understand for "start" and "stop," which means stop *right now*. If you are studying in a legitimate school of authentic martial arts, such a system will already be in place, clearly explained to and carefully observed by everyone, and inflexibly enforced by the instructors. If you are not working out in a school setting, it will be *your* responsibility to make, observe, and enforce the rules of safe practice.

Always keep safety as your primary consideration when working with training partners. Should a real-life bad actor compel you to use your tools in actual self-defense, however (and within the limits of common sense and the guidelines we discussed in "Situationally Appropriate Response"), safety is, frankly, a less critical consideration. As our school's motto says: *Caveat Aggressor* (Let the aggressor beware). If someone attacks you on the street, take care of business first and sort out the pieces later. If only one walks out of the alley, better you than him.

Bear in mind, as we discussed in the section on "Warrior Talk," that where it is not spelled out in the text, L = left, and R = right; A identifies the attacker, and D denotes the defender. Stay with your practice on a regular basis; your tools can be as good—and only as good—as the time, thought, and effort you put into building and maintaining them. Remember to make your workouts enjoyable—the best learning includes a little *fun!*

STRIKES

Strikes are a class of impact attacks including kicks, punches, slaps, and even sharp shoves and tackles. Hard blocks are often used as defensive strikes.

Generally, this class of attack is most commonly seen in male-on-male confrontations, and even gentlemen can, in some circumstances, come to blows. Punches and other blows with the fists are the most common strikes, but kicks are also frequently attempted. Less commonly encountered are elbow and knee strikes, and occasionally, hip checks and even head butts.

The best way to deal with most strikes is simply to get out of the way; don't be there when the strike arrives. Bruce Lee referred to this excellent tactic as *target denial*. We call it *getting off the line of attack*. The most efficient way to do this involves two skills: 1) correctly anticipating the intended strike (see "Improv-ing Your People-Reading Skills" in the Theory section); and then 2) taking a quick crescent step out of harm's way.

Your crescent step will move you to a position of relative (and temporary) safety, from which you can launch your response. As you move into your new stance, your arms come up into the guard position so that you can block, if necessary, and be well-positioned for a counter-capture, counter-strike, or other follow-up as required.

Because strikes move quickly, you'll need to be alert, to correctly "read" the intended strike, and to move fast enough in the right direction to stay a half-step ahead of the incoming attack. Several examples of common strike attacks and effective responses are presented in the pages that follow. Study them carefully and use them as springboards for your own practice.

STRIKE DEFENSE #1: CLOSE-RANGE BODY PUNCH

As with any incoming blow, close-range strikes to the body are best dealt with by not being where the strike is focused when it arrives—i.e., by *moving off the line of attack*. In illustration #1, D "reads" the intended incoming strike (in this case, an *empi* or elbow strike) and realizes that in order to deliver the attack

he intends, A will have to take a step toward her. D raises both hands for a double block, protecting the entire front of her torso. Correctly anticipating the step A must take to reach her and preparing for the circular path of his intended strike, . . .

. . . D carefully "reads" A's intention as he winds up to deliver a close-range strike—in this case, an *empi* to D's torso.

D simultaneously reaches forward to intercept and "absorb" A's elbow strike, at the same time taking a quick crescent step that mirrors the direction of A's incoming step . . .

. . . and the circular path of his incoming strike. These moves protect her from the brunt of the blow and position her to redirect the force of A's strike across his centerline.

Discussion

From the luxury of our armchair perspective, we note in looking at illustrations 5 and 6 as shown that D would have to stay alert for any attempted kicks or leg sweeps by the now-grounded A. If D does sense any residual belligerence, it is a simple matter to take a step to the side and kick A from the greater safety of that position, if necessary.

Keep in mind that the sequence shown is just one of any number of possibilities. As an example, once D had crossed A's arms and destroyed his balance as shown in illustration #4, she might just as easily have elected to grab his shoulders and pull him into a knee strike to the groin and/or a kick to the knee, and/or . . . well, you get the idea. There are many solutions to any given attack scenario—this sequence is just one possibility among them. Because *you* are the martial artist, *you* get to decide how the solution unfolds.

D has taken control of A's force, using his power to assist her in pushing his arms across his centerline. D is now well-positioned to easily push A's elbow up into and past his chin, . . .

. . . destroying his root (balance) and driving him over backward.

Depending on the circumstances of the attack, D may elect to step in and administer a follow-up move to ensure that the matter is concluded to her satisfaction.

HEAD PUNCH DEFENSE #1

Using the "reading" skills she developed from the Theory section of this book, D quickly determines that A intends a right-hand punch to her head. She decides this is not a good idea . . .

. . . and opts for a quick crescent step to A's R side (review "Crescent Steps" in the Techniques section). Note that, simultaneously with the step, D has raised both hands to block A's arm . . .

. . . and continues to guide the punch harmlessly forward and away from her. D could use any of a number of follow-up responses from the position shown in illustration #3. She could, for example, easily push downward on A's arm with her forward R hand and deliver a powerful eagle-wing backhand strike to A's unprotected face with her L hand. D could push A's arm across his chest, crossing his centerline and destroying his balance, while at the same time stepping with her L foot behind his R knee and, perhaps, pulling back on his L shoulder (or hair) from behind, dropping him to the ground. Kicks could follow, if necessary. There are any number of possible follow-ups, as D sees fit to end the conflict.

Discussion

The basic defense sequence shown here is direct and deceptively simple, and it has accomplished the immediate objective of keeping D safe from the intended initial punch.

It seems unlikely, however, from the safe remove of our armchair perspective, that this sequence, in and of itself, is going to be sufficient to conclude this confrontation. The attacker is still on his feet, and he is not disabled or even discomfited in any significantly dissuasive way.

Something more may well be needed. If A does pursue his attack, D will not have much time to ponder her next obvious question: "What now?"

The answer is *further follow-up moves,* strung together in sequences called *combinations.* Putting together effective, efficient defensive *combinations* requires ready access to a wide variety of defensive techniques and tools, and some experience and practice in working with them. This illustrates the importance of *practicing* the use of the tools in your "mental toolbox" with training partners.

Look carefully at D's position in illustration #3. Mentally put yourself in her place.

If A did not quit at this point, what would you do? Some suggestions have been given at #3 above, but there are many other possibilities too. As you practice working with the scenarios presented throughout this book, consider other options that you might use in different situations. Remember that *you,* as the defender, are the martial artist. You can't wait for Superman, Xena, or the cops to arrive— the hero is going to have to be *you.*

That means that *you* are the one who will decide what tools, techniques, and tactics to employ, and which sequences and combinations are going to work best for *you.*

PUNCH DEFENSE #1

It is said of most attacks that the best defense is simply not to be there when it comes in. This is certainly true of strikes, like the punch shown here. Being prepared to move quickly in the right direction to avoid and/or meet the attack depends on "reading" the situation correctly, accurately predicting what the attack will be, and where and when it is intended to land— so that you can be advantageously positioned when it arrives.

A's intentions seem pretty clear here, giving D plenty of advance warning about what is to come.

D's response to A's attempted right-lunge punch is a quick R crescent step inside A's punch, blocking as she steps. Note that D uses both hands to block and control A's punching arm . . .

. . . and immediately executes a "wrap trap," snaking her L arm over the top and then down and around A's punching arm, locking it tightly to her body, immobilizing the attack.

Discussion

Note that D keeps her R hand and arm (in this case, called the "off" or "free" arm) up throughout the entire sequence, as "cheap insurance" against any attempt A might make to grab onto her with his L arm (in order to save himself from falling), or against accidental kicks if his legs should fly up as he falls. D finishes in a strongly rooted ready stance, prepared to deliver any further follow-up (kicks, etc.) that she may deem necessary to conclude the confrontation to her satisfaction.

In a smooth, continuous motion, D steps strongly back to the left as she opens her arms to swing A around and off balance, . . .

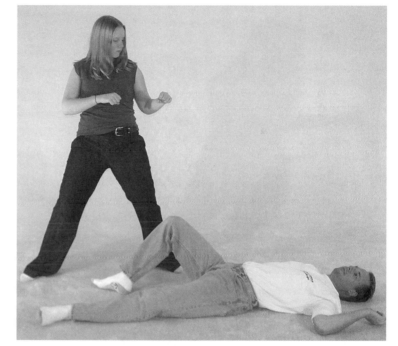

. . . dropping him backward to the ground.

GRABS AND CAPTURES

Most attacks by males against women begin with—and in many cases consist largely (and sometimes entirely) of—grabs and captures. These can be wrist or arm grabs intended to force the victim to move in some direction against her will, such as into a room, an alley, a car, and so on. The hair may be grabbed, or a purse, clothing, or any other portion of the anatomy.

Most grabs and holds are not, in and of themselves, dangerous, although what is intended to follow certainly can be. Generally, the captures themselves are intended to control, subdue, or intimidate, rather than immediately harm the victim, although they can cause sufficient fear or discomfort to prompt compliance with the attacker's demands. Slower than strikes, grabs afford the defender a bit more time to formulate and initiate a defensive response.

If you see an attempted capture coming soon enough, evasion is often possible simply by moving out of the trajectory of the incoming grab. Frequently, a light, slapping block will be sufficient to redirect an intended grab. Occasionally, a more powerful block is required. Once a capture has succeeded, and the attacker has secured a hold, it usually becomes necessary to either effect an escape or to turn the tables and use the attacker's hold against him (i.e., "stealing his power.") as a control to assist in the application of the desired defense.

Captures are frequently accompanied by pulling or pushing motions, which the defender can use to "turn the tables," co-opting or "stealing" the attacker's power to the defender's advantage. As Grandmaster Yun never tired of reminding us: *When pulled, follow; when pushed, fade.* This tactic is very frustrating for the attacker, who feels as if he is "fighting with fog." His own force is used to defeat him. This is part of the "secret" behind martial arts defense tactics, and it is why those techniques work so well, regardless of relative size and power.

REAR ARM GRAB DEFENSE #1

The rear arm grab shown here is a classic capture, probably the single most common arm grab in cases where the assailant is attempting to hustle the intended victim into a car, an alley, or elsewhere against the defender's will. Of the many ways to defeat this grab, the defense shown here is one of the simplest and most effective.

In Shindo, we call this technique the "grand wheel" escape, because of the large circle described by the defender's arm. As in all Shindo techniques, the wheel is powered not only by the arm but from the heels, using the power of the whole body.

A grabs D's arm from side or rear.

D takes a long step forward, breaking A's root, and begins raising her arm in a large opening circle.

As D's opening arm circle continues around, the leverage of the mechanics involved force A's grip open.

Discussion

Even a smaller defender using full-body power in the forward step shown at (2) can pull a larger attacker (or two) off balance long enough to complete the arm wheel escape. Leverage makes this escape effective, regardless of the relative size of the attacker and defender. Note the importance of invoking full-body power in the arm circle, involving the entire body, moving from the feet, not simply circling the arm from the shoulder.

The pivot back to face A (4) positions D to follow up if necessary with other techniques (e.g. kicks to knee, groin, or solar plexus, etc.) in order to be sure that the situation is resolved. Note at (5) that the centripetal force of D's large arm circle has propelled A's attacking arm across his centerline, again breaking his root (i.e., destroying his balance)—this time to his left. He has hardly had time to recover his balance from being pulled forward with D's initial step forward (2). Being out of balance robs A's power, to D's advantage.

D continues her opening arm circle and pivots to face A.

D is now free and ready to flee or follow up with a kick or other techniques at her option.

REAR ARM GRAB DEFENSE #2

Looking over her shoulder at the attacker, . . .

. . . D takes a quick L step back into A and raises her L arm, wrapping it up from behind and back down over the top of A's arm, breaking A's grip and counter-capturing A's arm.

Continuing to circle A's arm, D reinforces her grip by joining her hands together and pulling them tightly in to her own *t'an t'ien*, and she sinks her weight by dropping into a powerful horse stance (review "Stances" in the Techniques section).

Discussion

This counter-trap is usually sufficient to conclude these sorts of confrontations. If more persuasion is needed, many follow-up options are available—the arm lock, for example, makes it easy to tweak, dislocate, or even (if necessary) break A's elbow. A cobra kick could be employed in a forceful shove to roll A away, and so on. If the arm grab was from a stranger trying to pull D into a car, a room, alley, or other place against D's will, try to get a good look at A and immediately tell an adult or the police about the assault.

BREAST GROPE / SHOULDER "HUG"

Not all assaults are intended to harm the victim. Some, like this one—which can manifest as either a breast grope or, alternately, as a rough or overly powerful one-armed shoulder "hug"—are just plain rude and stupid, but socially unacceptable nonetheless. As we read in "Situationally Appropriate Response" in the Theory section, because no serious harm is intended, the response cannot legitimately inflict serious damage on the offender.

A bit of pain in the wrist and elbow lock may be justified, but serious damage—such as breaking or dislocating the arm—is probably not warranted for self-defense in this circumstance.

A drunken or otherwise socially impaired lout commits an uninvited social indiscretion.	He has chosen his victim unwisely; she is trained in self-defense. D clamps both hands over his offending hand, pinning it tightly against her momentarily while she . . .	. . . ducks beneath and under his arm, maintaining his hand tightly pinned against her as she steps behind him, placing her R hand behind his offending R elbow.	Maintaining the wrist pin as she stands back up, D pushes down on A's R elbow, driving him to his knees and extracting an apology and other follow-up as she deems suitable.

TWO ASSAILANTS—ARM GRAB

If there's anything more annoying than having to deal with some fool tugging on your arm uninvited, it's having to deal with *two* of them—at the same time. While this situation is less common than dealing with a solo jerk, it does happen. And, as intimidating as it may seem, the situation can be handled, if you keep your wits about you, remember the simple basics of your Shindo kinetic theory, and keep your defensive tools sharp with regular practice. Remember how unstable and weak even a very strong attacker becomes when you break his root? Goes double for two of 'em; compromise their balance, and they're yours. Let's watch how the defender in this situation handles these two rude poltroons.

1 D receives an uninvited and unwelcome offer she decides she can refuse.

Quickly sizing up the situation, she determines that she must break the root of both her assailants in order to stand a chance against their greater number, weight, and strength.

2 Imagine their surprise as D immediately takes a long, lurching step forward and, moving from the heels, in a very large circular motion raises her arms forward and up, just enough to break their balance, but circling smoothly enough that their grip is not broken—yet.

Discussion

D's big steps forward and back, accompanied by her large circling arm traps, are key in destroying the attackers' balance. This works because D is using her entire body weight and power against just one arm for each of the assailants. Care must be taken not to move so sharply or so far on the first step that the attackers lose their grip on D's arms; she has plans for them and is not ready to let them go just yet.

D's plans materialize soon enough as she completes her arm circle entrapment of the shoulders of both attackers and drops them down forward and in front of her (4), again using her whole-body power and dropping her full body weight into the drop as she completes her arm traps (3) and drives her arms (and the attackers) down (4). Should the head knock not work out to D's satisfaction, a number of other options arise once both attackers are on the ground. *Moo-rop* (knees) to faces comes to mind as one example, or she could simply slide her hands up to their wrists to raise their arms for face kicks, or pull any of a number of other tools from her self-defense toolbox, as she deems necessary to conclude the affair.

Immediately, before they can regain their bearings, D reverses direction, stepping back and circling her arms the other way—down, under, and then back up over their shoulders from behind, . . .

. . . trapping and then dropping them both forward in front of her. The weight of the attackers does 95% of the work, at D's direction. Often with this technique, the attackers' heads will crack together as they fall.

FRONT HAIR GRAB DEFENSE #1

This very common attack is often seen in "horseplay" and in "bullying" types of attacks, where misguided "teasing," annoyance, or harassment is the goal, and serious harm is not necessarily intended. Depending on the circumstances, a simple counter-capture will usually suffice for at least an initial response and will, in most cases, conclude the confrontation.

Discussion

A's interest in pursuing the confrontation will diminish markedly at this point, and D will be able to offer suitable admonishments and extract appropriate apologies with little further trouble. Any residual insufficiency in A's attitude can be corrected with the least bit of further pressure on the lock. In some cases, A may try to pull his hand and arm back toward himself, trying to get away from the pain of D's lock. D, however, is in a position of greatly superior leverage, and needs only to lean back a bit to pull A's arm straight out toward her, and his hand more tightly into her lock.

A frequent theme throughout this book, and in many of my lectures to students, is that the beauty of unarmed defensive controls of this sort lies precisely in the fact that they may be applied with as much—or as little—power as each situation demands.

If the hair-pull illustrated here was in fact

A grabs D's hair from the front—a bad idea. D immediately claps her hand over the top of the offending hand, pinning it tightly to her own forehead, preventing A from pulling on her hair.

D immediately reinforces her counter-capture with her other hand, tightly pinning A's offending hand so that he cannot withdraw it until she has finished with him.

Maintaining a tight pin on A's offending hand, D bends forward from the waist, pushing A's hand back against his wrist. Dropping her chin to her chest and breathing out, D pulls A's hand from her head, continuing to apply pressure against his wrist joint.

between friends and in fun, slight pressure, applied slowly, would decide the matter with no lasting harm. If, on the other hand, the attack was real and serious harm intended, the same playful tweak used on an unruly friend can, with the slightest increase in speed and pressure, turn instantly into disabling dislocations and/or fractures of fingers, wrist, and arm.

This versatility and potentially devastating effectiveness is why the self-defense techniques of traditional martial arts work so well for practitioners of any size and strength—and it is why it is so important to insist on control in class. When practicing with friends and fellow stu-

dents, always err on the side of caution. Rely on your partners' feedback to know when you've achieved control. Always let just enough be enough, and never go for more. When your training partners say quit, quit. Now.

Students at brown belt (intermediate) level in our schools are required to perform their judo techniques using just two fingers—or less; higher grades with one. Why? Because *good techniques do not require great force*—in fact, the better ones need very little, and the best use close (in some cases very close) to none. In martial arts applications, this "secret" is another facet of the many meanings behind the ancient teaching that *less is more.*

Quickly wrapping both of her thumbs around A's hand and deep into his palm just below the pads at the base of his fingers, still gripping with her fingers on the back of his hand, D uses both of her thumbs to push A's hand down and back against his wrist joint.

Continuing to put pressure on A's wrist, D sinks to one knee, maintaining the wrist lock to take A's head to the ground. Note that, in keeping with good Shindo practice, D keeps her back straight and does not lean forward toward A as he lies on the ground.

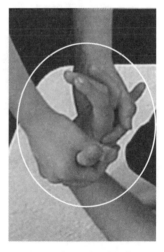

To complete the lock, D moves her thumbs from the center of A's palm to wrap them in a firm grip around his thumb and little finger, as shown.

REAR HAIR GRAB DEFENSE #1

Like the front hair grab, this common attack is often seen in situations where annoyance, rather than serious bodily injury, is intended. Depending on the circumstances, D could deliver a rear kick to groin or knee, or she could simply step back into A with, perhaps, an *empi* (elbow) strike, and so on. In this example, D clearly knows that this attack is an "annoyance" attack, more in the nature of horseplay than a life-threatening situation, and she does not wish to harm the attacker. She decides that a simple counter-capture will handle the situation. She may even have enough fun with the defense that she might forget to tell Mom about the incident!

1 As A grabs D's hair from the rear, she immediately claps her hand over the top of the offending hand, pinning it tightly to her own head, in order to prevent A from pulling on it, the little pest.

2 Reinforcing her counter-capture with both hands, A simply bends forward and turns to the rear, . . .

3 . . . maintaining a tight pin on A's offending hand and stepping behind him, taking his captured hand with her and (in this case, gently) bending his arm up behind his back, grabbing his collar, . . .

Discussion

Because the defense shown here is to a situation of horseplay rather than an attack intending serious harm, D moderated her response accordingly. Exactly the same technique, however, works just as well in more serious circumstances, when executed with a bit less gentleness and more authority. If required, for example, the arm can easily be pushed further up behind A's back, perhaps secured with a same-hand grab of a bit of A's clothing to stabilize the hold. If A continues to act belliger-ently or poses real danger, the arm and/or shoulder can easily be dislocated or broken if need be. If defending against a more serious attack, a defender could easily, from the control shown in illustration #4, step down with a cobra push-kick to the back of A's knee. With A on the ground, D could quickly trade the collar hold to grab a handful of hair and pull A's head back while pushing the arm still further up his back, and so on.

. . . and pulling back on his collar or shoulder while pushing his hand forward into the small of his back, keeping him off balance and well controlled.

LAPEL GRAB DEFENSE #1

Lapel grabs are one of the most common forms of grabbing attack. It is true that such assaults are occasionally performed by drunks or unpleasant relatives whose only intended follow-up is a wagging finger, a faceful of boozy breath, and perhaps some unintelligible argumentation, but generally such assaults should be taken as serious attacks until the defender determines otherwise. Watch carefully for what the other hand is doing—is a punch intended? Or worse, is a weapon involved? This is information you want to ascertain early on; review "Improving Your People-Reading Skills" in the Theory section of this book.

A grabs D's lapel, and D's initial "read" of his body language does not alert her to any very serious danger. His "off" (free) hand, for example, is not cocked to deliver a punch, and he apparently does not have a weapon. D therefore determines that a simple escape will suffice for at least an initial response. (She can always escalate her response.)

Reaching up to trap A's hand to her shoulder, D quickly turns away from A to face rearward, . . .

. . . and maintaining a tight pin on his captured hand, reaches up with her free hand to grab his collar, ear, or a handful of hair (with bald attackers, go for the collar), . . .

Discussion

Note: This book deals specifically with basic unarmed defense against unarmed attacks (luckily, still by far the most common sort of assaults, even in violent cultures like the U.S.). While we do share a few weapons defenses here, weapons attacks generally require spe-cialized training that is beyond the scope of this book. In fact, no book alone can prepare you for realistic defense against weapons attacks—for that you'll need to invest some serious time and effort in specialized classes under expert instructors.

. . . and pulls A over backward, . . .

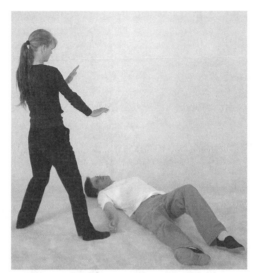

. . . dropping him to the rear and adopting an alert ready stance, positioning herself to deliver any kicks to ribs, head, or other follow-up.

FRONT WRIST GRAB

This very common attack can vary widely in intent, from misguidedly clumsy expressions of uninvited "friendliness" to worst-case attempts at outright abduction. D must "read" the situation carefully in order to gauge an appropriate response. There is an infinite number of responses, depending on the presentation (how aggressive does the intent appear to be?), location (an office party or a dark alley?), and circumstance (others present; all alone). In this case, A does not appear particularly aggressive; his "off" hand is not chambered for a punch or grab, and no weapon is in evidence. Let's assume that in this case, others are present, and it is daylight. D therefore determines that a simple release is all that is required, at least for the moment. She can always escalate her response, should the situation warrant stronger measures. Chances are that in this case, it won't.

A unwisely seizes D's hand, without invitation.

The presumption is unwelcome; D takes a long R step back, pulling A off balance, and simply turns her hand so that her palm (and his) faces upward. This requires no particular strength, because A is already off balance.

Discussion

In most cases of this type, the simple fact that D has secured a release and seized the initiative from A so quickly and effectively (and with such apparent ease) usually effects prompt and marked improvement in A's attitude. Not only has D easily evaded A's attempted capture, but she has caused him to look and feel foolish as he stumbles forward, trying to recover his balance. The belligerent personality types who attempt such assaults generally reflect surprisingly brittle egos, and the least discouragement is often enough to persuade them to quit the scene rather than continue their embarrassment or risk further punishment.

D continues to turn her hand in a circle, cutting down to the outside of A's hand (past A's thumb) with a *shuto* ("sword hand"). Review the *shuto* in the Techniques section. This simple step and hand circle completes the release, and it is accomplished so quickly that A is still pitching forward out of balance. D is ready, in a solid stance, to meet him with an appropriate response if he fails to check himself before colliding into her.

FRONT SHOULDER GRAB

On occasion, an attacker may not realize that he has inadvertently grabbed not just one, but two people. The attacker shown here, however, is soon to discover, unhappily, that this particular soon-to-be mom is also a warrior spirit with more than enough training and experience to ruin his day, in many creative ways. As with the front wrist grab, there are a great many effective responses, depending on the situation. Pay close attention to all of A's body language, including what the feet are up to, and most particularly to what is happening with the off hand.

Is it holding a knife, perhaps, or is it configured into a fist? Or, as in this series of illustrations, is it simply held in a fairly neutral position? The neutral position and lack of weapon are good signs, indicating that this particular attacker is not thinking too far ahead (usually the case with those who engage in this type of behavior). This works to D's advantage—when dealing with bad guys, those without a specific agenda usually require less time and effort to process.

This grab can range in intent from misplaced "joking" to a serious assault. Be sure when "reading" this type of attack not to fall into the trap of focusing too narrowly on A's eyes, face, or hands. Instead, adopt a broad gaze (what we call "gazing to the horizon"), allowing you to take in the "big picture."

Discussion

D's response in this case is quick, simple, and highly effective; note how severely out of balance A's posture is torqued at position #3. Because D is imminently expecting, she may be less inclined, in this case, to employ some of the more acrobatic responses she might prefer when not so encumbered.

She can very easily move from the stance shown in illustration #3 into any number of follow-up moves. The lock as shown is set up to require the slightest push of another inch or two to dislocate or break A's elbow, wrist, or shoulder.

Alternately, it would be the work of a moment, for example, for D to place her L foot against the joint of A's near (R) knee, and then step forward with a soft cobra push-kick to drive him to the ground. A hair less soft on the cobra kick, and the knee is dislocated or broken.

D immediately takes control of the situation by very firmly pinning the offending hand to her shoulder or chest with her R hand, so that A cannot easily or quickly remove it until she is done working her magic. D then steps in L and places her L hand so that she can push against the joint of A's elbow.

Gliding easily, D steps in even further, cranking against the elbow joint with sufficient authority to secure a suitable adjustment in A's attitude. It will be shortly forthcoming. Don't get so busy pushing on the elbow, worrying about where your feet are placed, or being amused at the funny noises A will be making that you forget to maintain pressure on your hand pin. It is critical, in order to make this lock work effectively, to keep the attacking hand firmly clamped until you are done with it.

HEADLOCK DEFENSE #1

The enduringly popular (and embarrassingly stupid) headlock is easily dealt with. As is true of two-handed grabs in general, this type of attack immobilizes the attacker just as effectively as it does the intended victim and, as we shall see, puts him at a greater disadvantage if his "victim" is versed in even the rudi-

ments of self-defense. Because the headlock can act—even unintentionally—as a choke hold, D will remember to breathe *out* and not in (see "Chokes"). Luckily, the release from this type of headlock is easily and quickly effected with this technique.

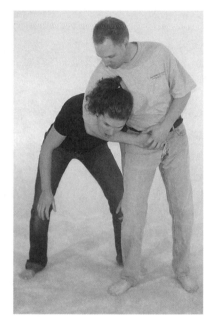

A unwisely pulls D into a classic front standing headlock.

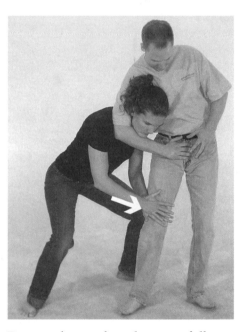

D remembers to breathe powerfully *out* as she sinks into a strong horse stance.

To effect an immediate release from the hold, D simply places both hands just above A's kneecap and pushes straight back against the joint and down, . . .

Discussion

Note that, in the case of this classic headlock, A is standing nearly upright, with his legs fairly straight. Sometimes, however, the attacker will bend forward or squat down so that his knees are bent forward, making this defense very difficult or unworkable, because in that case, D would likely not be able to force A's knee backward. Often in such situations, the attacker's knees are either straight or only slightly bent.

In cases where the attacker's knees are more deeply bent, as in a slight squat, D must take one additional preliminary step. In such cases, it will usually be necessary for D to first apply pressure with a palm (or elbow) just *below* A's knee joint, pushing back against the joint in order to straighten out A's knee. From there, D can proceed as shown.

. . . driving A backward to the ground. Depending on the amount of force D uses, A's leg may be simply tweaked, dislocated, or broken. D's strong horse stance will prevent A from pulling her down with him as he falls backward.

CHOKES AND STRANGLEHOLDS

Chokes and strangleholds are a specialized type of grab or capture, and they are among the scariest and most dangerous types of assaults. For that reason, many people are uncomfortable even discussing this unpleasant subject, and shy away from studying how to deal with this class of attacks. While the aversion is understandable, it is a mistake, for unfortunately, these attacks are common.

Certainly if someone has their hands—or a rope—around your neck, you need to react quickly, decisively, and effectively. Most people, however, instinctively react to these types of attack in precisely the wrong way.

Virtually all choke attacks fall into one of two types: a manual choke (using the hands) or strangulation by ligature (with a cord or garrote of some kind). In either case, unless your attacker happens to be an accomplished *thuggee*, well-versed in *shime waza* (techniques of strangulation), the commonly held misconception that unconsciousness—let alone death—will result in a matter of a few seconds is greatly overblown. The truth is that *if you react properly and know what to do*, you will have sufficient time to escape from the choke hold or attempted strangulation well before the onset of unconsciousness, and to deliver an effective and decisive response.

Virtually all untrained victims subjected to a choke or stranglehold immediately panic, reach up to grab the wrists of the attacker, and instinctively try to *breathe in*. This, of course, does not work, and in fact only exacerbates the situation. Because the windpipe is constricted, the victim chokes, and, realizing they can't breathe, most succumb to yet further panic. Attempts to push or pull on the attacker's hands or wrists are invariably futile and waste precious time and energy.

The correct response in such situations is completely counter-intuitive, but here it is: *don't try to breathe in—breathe out*. This only works, however, if you do it properly, which is very slowly and forcefully, from *t'an t'ien*.

Because your lungs have much more power on exhale than when you are inhaling, you will be able, in most cases, to breathe out. Not freely, of course, if your windpipe is constricted, but you will be able to breathe out to some degree nevertheless.

Reacting in this way rather than trying to

inhale, you will not choke, which will buy you a little extra time in which to avoid panic, and to keep a clear head as you launch your counter-attack.

Pull your chin tightly down onto your chest, tighten your diaphragm, and draw your elbows in to your sides, making tight fists with both hands. All of these actions tighten the musculature used in respiration, enabling you to resist the effect of the attempted choke. Because you are able to keep a clear head, you will not waste your time or energy on futile attempts to pry your attacker's hands, or vainly tugging on the rope. Knowing where both of his hands are (on your neck, or to the sides if he is using a garrote), frees your attention to focus more effectively on attacking other, unguarded targets, such as his eyes and groin, in order to create a distraction as a set-up for your escape.

Attacking the assailant's eyes and/or groin will produce an immediate loosening of his grip (if using his hands) or, if a cord is used, of the stranglehold. If a garrote was used in the attack, pull it loose immediately while the attacker is busy reacting to your initial counter-attack, and then execute termination of the conflict with techniques of your choice.

NOTE: We strongly recommend extreme caution when practicing these defenses, and especially when practicing the garrote attacks. The very rare Iron Neck *kung* is extremely helpful in this regard, but not more than a handful of people in the world currently are qualified to conduct this type of training. It is *not* safe for amateur exploration. Those interested in this highly specialized area of study may contact us at our website for further information.

STANDING FRONT CHOKE #1

The standing front choke is one of the most common choke attacks. While it can be very scary, it is actually quite easily dealt with.

Discussion

D's big step back with her L leg (2) is key: A won't be able to let go of her quickly enough to avoid being pulled forward and off balance. Because fear of falling is "hard-wired" into human beings, saving his balance now eclipses his interest in attacking D; his choke hold relaxes. D's follow-up hammer strike (3) swings A's arm out, leaving him wide open for D's side kick to the solar plexus (5).

This admittedly severe response can, in some cases, be fatal, so we don't advocate its use in casual situations. Do not hesitate to use it in a choke attack, however. Because such attacks can be dangerous, even fatal, such harsh responses are legitimately warranted. In cases of potentially lethal attacks, act quickly and decisively to ensure that the attacker is sufficiently disabled to preclude any further aggression.

D remembers to override her natural instinct to try to breathe in (which will not work) and instead breathes strongly *out* from *t'an tien*. This helps her avoid panic and keep a clear head, and buys her valuable seconds in which to formulate and then launch her defensive counter-attack.

D launches her counter-attack with an initial step back (2), using her whole body weight to break A's root. As A lurches forward to try to save his balance, D steps back in quickly, raising her hand in a lightning-fast *biu ji* strike to A's eyes. The *biu ji* strike invokes the startle response, and A's head jerks back, trying to get away from the eye jab, distracting him and further disrupting his balance.

A's grip on D's neck relaxes as his attention turns to his new priority: saving his balance. Keeping her hips and shoulders in a straight line, D pivots to deliver a powerful closing hammer to A's arm as she breaks completely free.

Continuing her pivot, D turns to look over her L shoulder, shifting weight to her R leg in preparation for her finishing technique, . . .

. . . which she has decided will be a powerful L side kick to A's solar plexus. A's appetite for further aggression will evaporate as he heads to the ground. D may then easily deliver additional follow-up she deems necessary.

STANDING FRONT CHOKE #2

A perennial favorite with bad guys who are not big thinkers (that would be most of them), the standing front choke practically begs for any number of effective defensive responses. Consider that, with both of his hands immobilized—on the defender's neck—the attacker has left himself wide open and effectively defenseless. This most common choke attack is therefore very easily dealt with in any number of ways. Feel free to borrow the techniques and tactics shown in this sequence, but also use your imagination to envision other responses you might make in similar situations.

A attacks D frontally, wrapping both hands around her neck in an attempt to strangle her.

D, remembering (as in all choke situations) not to try to breathe in, but instead to breathe strongly *out* from *t'an t'ien*, steps forward into A while raising her arms up between his arms, as if she were diving into a pool.

Raising her whole body weight in a smooth upward thrust of both arms, she separates her hands as they rise up past A's face, invoking A's startle response and breaking his choke hold as his arms fly out to the sides.

Discussion

In this sequence, D has decisively defeated A's attempted strangle, broken one or both of his collar bones, broken his nose, might just as easily have kneed his groin, and dumped him to the dirt—all in considerably less than five seconds. Considering the damage he has sustained, A may very well take a while to recover from shock, let alone from his injuries. But because choke holds are potentially so dangerous, even fatal, they must be taken seriously and dealt with unhesitatingly. No apology is due to anyone who grabs you by the neck without permission.

D now reverses the upward arc of her arm swing and drives them back down, again using body weight behind the strike, to drop both hands in the *shuto* or "sword hand" ("karate chop") configuration heavily onto A's exposed clavicles (collar bones).

While A is still dazed from the blow to his clavicles, and since her hands are already handily placed on A's shoulders anyway, D quickly wraps her fingers around the back of A's neck, the better to pull his head forward into a head butt to the nose. (Be sure to review the information on correct head butt delivery in the Techniques section.) Not shown here is another technique that would work well at this juncture: D could easily raise one knee sharply up into A's groin—just another of the many handy options to keep in mind.

The rest, like A, is already history. D simply takes a further powerful step forward and shoves A forcefully to the ground.

STANDING REAR CHOKE DEFENSE #1

There is any number of effective ways to respond to this common type of choke attack.

As with any choke attack, it can be scary, and it is critically important that D remembers to override her natural instinct to try to breathe in and instead breathes strongly *out* from *t'an tien*. This diminishes choking, helps to prevent panic, and buys valuable seconds in which to launch a defense.

D, breathing strongly out from *t'an tien,* takes a long R step forward, pulling A off balance, . . .

. . . and then, keeping her hips and shoulders in a straight line (review "Carry the Water" in the Techniques section), raises her L arm in an opening arc over both of A's arms at the elbows, . . .

Discussion

Keep in mind that D can use any of the self-defense tools at her command in any way she thinks necessary. What follow-up moves might she access? From the position shown in illus-tration #6, she could easily move to step on top of A's instep, raise her knee into his groin, cobra kick to the knee, and so on.

. . . and continuing down in a wrap trap, . . .

. . . securely pins both of A's arms.

She then steps back into A again with her R foot and drives a powerful R *empi* (elbow) strike into A's ribs.

STANDING REAR CHOKE DEFENSE #2

1 This is another simple and very effective defense against a standing rear choke attack. Remembering to breathe *out,* not in, . . .

2 . . . D takes a long R step forward, pulling A off balance, and then, as shown in Standing Rear Choke Defense #1, D steps back L into A and with her R hand delivers an opening block against the joint of A's near elbow.

3 Maintaining pressure against A's elbow in order to steady herself, D places the sole of her foot just above A's knee . . .

4 . . . and steps back and down through the joint, breaking A's knee.

Discussion

As distressing as the prospect of the knee break shown at illustration #4 is, and it is a severe response indeed, attempted choke and strangle attacks are potentially very dangerous, even lethal, and a broken leg, while painfully debilitating for a time, does not kill.

An unhappy fact of self-defense is that it is sometimes necessary to do something distasteful. It is helpful in this respect to keep in mind that it is the attackers who bring such consequences upon themselves, and not the choice of the defenders.

REAR ARM BAR CHOKE DEFENSE #1

Probably the second most popular choke attack, right behind the standing front choke, the rear arm bar is very scary, and when applied against an untrained victim, it can be lethal.

As with any choke attack, it is critically important that D remembers to override her natural instinct to try to breathe in (which will not work) and instead breathes strongly *out* from *t'an tien*. This helps her avoid panic and keep a clear head, and buys her valuable seconds in which to formulate and launch her defense.

As A applies a rear arm bar choke, D quickly lowers her weight (and her concentration) to *t'an t'ien*, breathing *out* to avoid choking and panic.

The natural reaction to this type of hold is to attempt to pull out and away (i.e., towards the offending wrist and hand).

D, however, knows that the correct response is to move counter-intuitively, lowering her chin down into the fold of A's elbow, and taking control of his attacking arm. At the same time, she takes a strong lurching step in that direction.

Maintaining control of A's elbow to prevent him from letting go before she's finished with him, D delivers a powerful rear *empi* (elbow) strike to A's solar plexus, . . .

. . . followed immediately by a descending fist hammer to A's groin (remembering to drop her whole body weight slightly at the knees to power the blow, of course).

D then raises her whole body weight into the rising eagle wing she delivers to A's nose. These three strikes occur in very quick succession, . . .

. . . leaving A disoriented, and in the onset of shock as D pivots R and raises A's arm for her fourth strike, an opening *empi* (elbow) blow to his ribs.

Moving quickly before A can recover, D snugs her R hip into A's R hip and sets him up for a front drop (review the section on forward drops for detail).

Maintaining a proper grip on A's attacking hand and just above his elbow, D keeps her back straight, using proper drop technique.

A's appetite for further aggression will evaporate as he heads to the ground, and D, keeping her back straight to avoid being pulled down on top of A, . . .

Discussion

Remember that you can instantly access any tools you like from the arsenal in your mental toolbox, and apply them in any sequence that gets the job done. Nobody tells a painter which brush to use next, or how; and there's a reason these are called martial *arts*.

Some of these responses are admittedly a bit severe, but the attack was an attempted strangle—potentially life-threatening attacks must be taken seriously. Do not hesitate to use whatever tools and techniques you deem necessary in a choke attack. Additional follow-up may or may not be required; should the attacker still appear unconvinced, for example, it would be very easy and quick for D to go ahead and break his arm over her knee as shown in illustration #10. From there, perhaps, D might raise A's arm and deliver a kick to the ribs.

10

. . . elects to maintain control of A's arm, levering his elbow over her knee for an easy arm break, or other additional follow-up as needed.

GROUNDWORK

Groundwork consists of grappling and wrestling once the combatants have gone to the ground, which very commonly happens in many types of assaults, including rapes and other serious attacks, regardless of gender.

This is where you don't want things to go but, because they so often do, it's advisable to be familiar with a variety of ways to deal with such eventualities.

GROUNDWORK DEFENSE #1: STRADDLE STRANGLE, BOTH ARMS FREE

One of the most common and potentially most dangerous types of ground attack is the straddle strangle, in which the attacker (A) sits astride the defender (D), choking the intended victim with both hands. Luckily, the techniques of Shindo provide a very effective defense to this situation. Remember that A's balance or "root" is stable in the sitting position only so long as he remains sitting upright. His balance becomes unstable at the moment he leans forward to wrap his hands around his intended victim's neck. In this position, the only thing holding him up is his arms and hands. When D knocks those props out from under him, A's balance is destroyed, and over he goes. Once A begins to fall, D simply guides his fall in the desired direction, keeping a strong grasp on A to follow as he tumbles, "riding" A's energy up into the superior (top) position, and administering a finishing *coup de grace*.

Typical attack, with A mounted astride his intended victim, both hands around her neck. At this point, A's job is to keep her wits about her. Her life may well depend on her ability to fend off any shock engendered when she was slammed to the ground, and upon remembering to resist the natural impulse to try to breathe in, instead breathing powerfully *out* from *t'an t'ien*. This buys her a few moments to clear her head, avoid choking and forestall panic, and prepare to deliver her response.

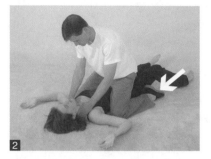

The response begins as D, *continuing to breathe out*, slides one foot (her right foot, in these illustrations) in toward her buttocks, bringing her right knee up behind A's back.

Still breathing out, D brings both hands together as if diving into a pool and then interlaces her fingers, joining her hands together for greater power as she brings them up between A's arms.

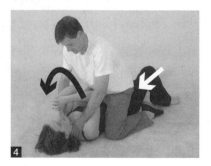

D continues to bring her arms up deeper inside A's arms, positioning her elbows inside the crooks of A's elbows, and bringing her right leg up tight behind A's back, planting her right foot firmly on the ground.

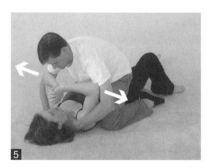

Bracing her elbows inside the crook of A's elbows, A "spreads her wings" in order to collapse A's elbows outward. This breaks A's stranglehold, and D can take a quick breath, setting her up to breathe strongly *out* again as she completes her defense.

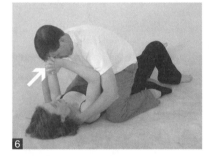

As D collapses A's elbows outward, he begins to pitch forward, on top of A—but A knows this is coming and is ready, using her interlaced "double fist hammer," to strike upward sharply to A's nose. This provokes several immediate reactions from A. His eyes will close involuntarily and begin to water copiously, his nose may begin to bleed, and, forgetting all about his choke hold, he will try to sit back up away from D's fists.

Too late—D already has other plans for him. Grabbing with both hands to secure his hair, collar, an ear, or whatever else is handy, D pulls down with one hand and shoves up with the other to push and pull A over to the side. The importance of planting the "pushing foot" flat on the ground cannot be stressed too strongly, for without the greater power of the legs, it will be much more difficult to roll A off to the side. Because in this case D has pulled her right leg up behind A, she will push and buck upward with her right leg and hip, at the same time pushing up with her right arm, while simultaneously pulling down with her left arm, to roll A off to her left side. (By pulling the left leg up initially, the process can be reversed.)

Either way, over he goes, with D retaining a strong grip with both hands, . . .

. . . the better to use A's fall in order to "ride" his energy up into the superior (top) position, from whence D can easily administer a suitable *coup de grace*.

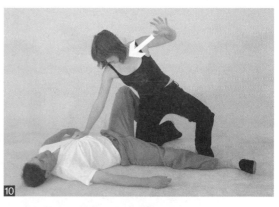

In this illustration, it appears that D is preparing a palm heel strike to A's nose, solar plexus, or groin—or perhaps all of the above. Remembering to use full-body power, D will use not just arm strength alone but will capitalize on the advantage of the superior position she has taken by adding a little body weight to each finishing strike she decides to deliver.

WEAPON DEFENSES

The class of individual who uses weapons in attacks against unarmed victims is even lower and more cowardly than those who at least conduct their assaults *mano a mano*. Obviouly attacks involving weapons require an entirely different level of response.

When dealing with bare-hand attacks, care is taken to tailor the response to the level of intended harm, with an eye to doing as little damage to the attacker as necessary to control the situation.

The vermin who use weapons to attack unarmed victims do not warrant such consideration. If a weapon is involved, you must assume that deadly harm is intended, and you are fully justified in those circumstances in using whatever force is necessary to neutralize the attack.

Everyone in our self-defense classes is invited to bring a "what if" scenario to each class, and we work out several responses, deciding which ones work best for each student. Some of these are based on real-life experiences, some on things people have heard or read about, and a few on lively imaginations.

On one occasion, a student asked, "What if the bad guy is standing twenty feet away from you, and he's armed with an Uzi [machine gun]?" (I'm not making this up. Somebody really did ask this question in class—with a straight face.) "In that case," I replied, "I would comply with their demands." The student, unsatisfied with that response, persisted: "But what if that didn't work, and he still wanted to shoot you?" "In that case," I told her, "you would probably have no alternative but the KYAG response." She looked puzzled. "KYAG?" "Yes—Kiss it Goodbye."

This got a good laugh from the rest of the class, but the student who had posed the question was not amused. Perhaps having seen too many movies, she was under the unrealistic impression that martial artists can handle every conceivable attack situation. Unfortunately, that only happens in Hollywood.

That said, and while it is true that armed attacks are the "worst-case" scenario for unarmed defenders, there are nevertheless some commonly encountered hand weapons—and fairly standard types of armed attacks—that traditional martial arts self-defense tactics can handle. While this is a particularly ugly topic, and we especially hope you never run into any of these situations in real life, we'll take a look at a few of them, just in case.

One last note on weapons defense: those properly trained in martial arts and in realistic self-defense always try to use the minimum amount of force necessary to conclude any given confrontation. And, while this principle also applies, so far as is practicable, those who attack others using weapons must understand that in so doing, they leave much less room for error, and that smaller margin necessarily works against the attacker in such cases. In other words, if defense of your own life or the lives of others requires the use of severe—even deadly—force, so be it.

STICK/CLUB DEFENSE #1

Stick and/or club attacks are among the most common (and surely the oldest) type of weapon attacks. While a stick or club attack can come from any direction, opening (backhand) or closing, and on a horizontal, oblique, or vertical plane, the most common attack of this type is the overhead vertical attack shown here.

Discussion

Remember in any attack situation to "read" the circumstances and tailor your response appropriately. In this case, the attacker is smaller and lighter than the defender, and the weapon she wields is not terribly dangerous. D's response might have been a bit more forceful if, say, A were a larger and more threatening opponent, or if she were attacking with a crowbar, baseball bat, or machete instead of a smallish stick.

1

A approaches with the obvious intent of hitting D with an overhead strike, which D declines to accept, . . .

2

3

4

Here again, D has taken control of the weapon and could easily unload a damaging counter-strike, but under the circumstances of this particular incident, he has determined instead that a "softer" response will suffice, and simply pushes A's head gently down and away.

. . . opting instead for a quick crescent step to the inside, where he is easily able to block the strike as it descends. Note the importance of the placement of D's block; he has not blocked on the stick itself, but on A's hand where it joins the stick. A's wrist is softer to block than the hard stick, and because it is closer to A's body, it is moving more slowly than the middle or end of the stick. Most of us have had the experience while carrying something of accidentally bumping our hand or fingers against a chair, doorway, or other impediment, and having the object we were carrying flip unintentionally out of our grasp.

D is capitalizing on the same principle here as he coordinates his block on A's wrist with pulling the stick easily out of A's hand. D has determined in this case (possibly because A is smaller and not as much a threat as a larger attacker might be) to block with his R hand and use his L hand to simply disarm A by pulling the stick out of her hand. Had D determined that a more aggressive defense was needed, he could just as easily have blocked, for example, with his L hand, and used his R hand to strike A in the face, pull her over backward by the hair, and so on.

KNIFE DEFENSE #1

A grabs D's lapel with his L hand and threatens her with a knife in his R.

While staying acutely aware of the location of the knife, D broadens her gaze to include all of A's body, and sinks her weight to *t'an tien*, breathing out to remain calm. Quickly determining what her response will be, . . .

. . . D pins A's L hand to her lapel with her L hand and takes a quick L step back to break A's root, followed immediately with a quick R crescent step to A's L side, placing her R hand behind A's elbow to keep A's body between her and the knife. In order to stab D, A would now have to cross his own centerline, which is prevented by the pressure against his elbow. D must take care not to relax the control secured by her tight pin on A's captured L hand.

Maintaining the lapel pin, D pushes against A's elbow, driving him to his knees, . . .

. . . and orders A to throw the knife a safe distance away.

Discussion

D must use clear, strong, and unequivocal commands when ordering A to throw the knife away, and she must watch that he does not throw it in any direction he can get to in a hurry. When practicing this technique, we often use the command (in a loud, stern voice), "Throw the knife toward me!" On paper, this sounds like a bad idea, but in practice, because D has A well controlled, on the ground, and a good lock on his arm, he cannot clearly target her when tossing the knife. The command is short and simple, and D will remain spry enough on her feet to move a leg out of the way if it looks like the knife might take a bad bounce. The remote chance of the inconvenience of a bad bounce (you can kick it aside) is worth getting the knife away from A and closer to a spot where D can recover it quickly once she lets go of A.

D will let go of A's arm only after being sure that he has been safely "decommissioned," at least temporarily. In this case, she has several options from the position of advantage shown at (4). Obvious possibilities include breaking A's captured arm (by pushing sharply against the elbow joint while maintaining the pin on his L wrist), and then, perhaps, using her hold on his arm to aid in her own balance, turning towards A and administering a kick or knee to the head or face, knocking him out or at least stunning him long enough for her to retrieve the knife.

As unpalatable as these techniques are, by employing a weapon in his attack, A has really left D no alternative. Anyone who attacks an unarmed target with a weapon should not expect to get off with a slap on the wrist.

IV. APPENDICES

A VERY BRIEF HISTORY OF UNARMED SELF-DEFENSE

Many modern schools and "styles" of martial arts borrow the most useful insights and practical techniques from a wide variety of traditional systems. Tao-Zen Ryu Shindo, the martial art system on which this book is based, derives from this eclectic model.

Shindo is built on the best tactics, techniques, and philosophies of several ancient classical martial traditions, including Ch'uan Fa (var. Kung Fu, Kenpo), Karate/Taekwondo; Jujitsu/Judo; and Hapkido/Aikido. In order to lend historical perspective to the lineage from which the theories and practices of Shindo have evolved, let us examine—very briefly—each of the principal ancestral traditions that have contributed to the development of modern-day Shindo.

THE ANCESTRAL ARTS
CH'UAN FA / KENPO
In about AD 520, an Indian monk named Bodhidharma (Ta Mo to the Chinese) traversed the Himalaya from India, arriving at the Shaolin monastery in Honan province, China. There he devised a series of exercises for the monks, which he called *shih pa lo han sho,* later known simply as *Lo Han,* or the "Eighteen Hands" (postures). These are considered by many to be the foundation of what eventually became Ch'uan Fa, also called Kenpo or "Kung Fu."

It is from this early Buddhist tradition that this school of Chinese martial arts became associated with the ideals of internal strength (*Ch'i*—var: Qi, Ki) and non-violence (control, but with minimal destruction). It is fairly safe to say that this tradition, spread as peripatetic monks and sailors traveled throughout the Orient, informed and influenced virtually all other Oriental styles.

JiuJitsu / JUDO
JiuJitsu is a generic name for ancient Japanese wrestling and throwing arts. As with all truly martial arts, JiuJitsu was originally a life-and-death battle art, used when combatants closed to arm's-length range.

As an unarmed form of combat, it offered

143

the great advantage of permitting less-than-lethal power to be employed, affording the option of capturing prisoners alive. Toward the close of the 19th century, Japan's Jigoro Kano updated JiuJitsu and modified some of its techniques into a (usually) non-lethal sport that he called Judo, meaning the "gentle way."

HAPKIDO / AIKIDO

In about AD 540, a short generation after the advent of Ta Mo in the Shaolin monastery, another Buddhist monk, named Won Kwang, is recorded as promulgating a martial art among the Koreans. It is even possible that Won Kwang studied directly with Ta Mo at the Shaolin temple.

Be that as it may, let us leave this lawless era and fast-forward to World War II, when a young Japanese lad named Morihei Ueshiba was developing a new synthesis from several earlier influences, including Ch'uan Fa and the "hard" northern-Japan style known as *Daito Ryu* JuJitsu, merging them with spiritual insights derived from ancient Zen and Taoist philosophical roots. Ueshiba formalized his synthesis into the art known today as "Aikido." "Hapkido" is simply the Korean pronunciation of the Japanese word "Aikido." Both systems stress "blending" with the opponent and turning the aggressor's strength to the defender's advantage.

TAEKWONDO / KARATE

As with Hapkido and Aikido, there are many similarities between Karate and Taekwondo. "*Kara-te*" is an Okinawan term that was changed from an earlier translation meaning "Chinese hand" to mean "empty hand" by the "father of modern Karate," an Okinawan school teacher named Gichin Funakoshi. Taekwondo is a name coined by a Korean general, Choi Hong Hi, in 1954. Early on, Taekwondo was often called "Korean karate," even by Korean practitioners. The names translate similarly: Karate, as Funakoshi used it, means "empty hand" (i.e., unarmed techniques), and Taekwondo translates roughly as "hand foot way"—essentially the same thing. Both, and particularly the styles that have most directly influenced the development of Tao-Zen Ryu Shindo, are regarded as "hard-style" impact-based striking arts.

QI GONG / CH'I KUNG

China is also home to the ancient practice of *Ch'i Kung (Qi Gong)*. Breathing is the channel for Qi, and the study and practice of Qi Gong focuses on the practice of deep and deliberate breathing, along with the judicious development and conscious employment of the vital energy created in self-defense and, indeed, in all of life's pursuits.

TAO-ZEN RYU SHINDO: MARTIAL ART AND PHILOSOPHY FOR THE TWENTY-FIRST CENTURY

The Tao-Zen Ryu Shindo system of martial art, a modern synthesis of many of the best and most effective principles of each of the traditional arts briefly examined above, was founded by Master J.G. Townsend during the waning years of the last century.

It takes many years to develop qualified instructors, but the system, originating in the Seattle area of Washington State, is gradually becoming more widely available as students begin assuming teaching duties and spreading the art to other areas.

Contact us at:
The Tao-Zen Academy
P.O. Box 1395
Poulsbo, Washington 98370
e-mail: info@tao zen.com
or visit us at our website: tao-zen.com

FINDING THE RIGHT SCHOOL FOR YOU

The two questions most frequently asked by people considering martial arts study are "Which is the best martial art?" and "What should I look for in a good school?" The most useful answer to both of these questions is that the best style and school for you is the one that best suits *you*. Considering the great investments in time, effort, and money that one expects to expend in such specialized education, prudence dictates that the choice of school and instructor should be very carefully researched before any commitment is made.

A good place to begin is a close look inside your own head and heart to ascertain what your true goals and objectives are. Write them down, in descending order of importance. How this list looks will help define the best school and system of instruction for you.

Once you've clearly defined your personal

objectives, begin visiting schools in your area to check them out. Many schools have regularly scheduled hours on certain days set aside for first-time visitors; others encourage "drop-ins" anytime. The courteous prospective student will call ahead to ascertain what times are convenient to the school and instructor one wishes to visit.

Time set, one should arrive promptly as scheduled. It is customary in most martial arts schools to remove one's shoes upon entering (visitors are usually allowed to hang onto their socks).

If a class is in progress when you arrive, be seated quietly along the wall nearest the door you entered (or on chairs or benches, of course, if you can get to them unobtrusively) and wait. The instructor or a senior student will soon approach to inquire of your business. If classes are not in session when you arrive, someone should be present, either in the classroom or in the office, to meet with you.

Get your "antennae" up; trust your intuition. What is the "atmosphere" of the school? How does it "feel"? Do the students working out look happy? Do these seem to be the sort of folks you'd enjoy spending a good deal of your time with for the next several years?

Every properly trained martial artist should have a deep understanding of the importance of *respect,* and this goes double for instructors. If you sense the slightest rudeness, faintest men-

ace, or least condescension, thank them for their time, take your wallet, and walk.

Any "guarantees" of eventual black belts or of "fast-track" promotions should prompt the deepest suspicion. No legitimate school can guarantee that you will eventually qualify for a black belt, any more than the local university can guarantee that you will eventually earn a degree, and there are no shortcuts in legitimate martial arts.

There are exceptions to every rule, but generally, a young, healthy student in very good shape, willing to work very hard and regularly, could conceivably earn a legitimate black belt in as little as four or five years. Most folks, however, should regard three to five years as a bare minimum, and five to six or seven is much more realistic. Ten or more is not unheard of. Besides, why be in a hurry? Once on the path, you will find that the real martial arts are the journey of a lifetime, rather than a destination.

Be sure that the school's class schedule will work for you. Assuming that you can budget the time, an ideal training schedule will allow for classes at least every other day. Training every day is a bit much for most people, but you don't want to go a great deal longer than two days in a row without practice. Many trainers regard every other day as ideal.

Rely on your intuition; do you feel comfortable with this instructor? Does his or her style appeal to you? Do they seem genuinely interested in you and your goals, or are you sensing that all they're really looking for is your billfold?

Legitimate martial arts instructors work very hard for many years to establish their credentials, but these can be difficult to check. Like doctors, lawyers, and other professionals, the better teachers post their certifications in plain and even prominent view, and welcome students to examine them.

Unfortunately, anyone can print up a certificate, buy a black belt, and hang out a shingle. Only those in the legitimate martial arts community really know who is authentically qualified and who is not.

Although such information is rarely easy to obtain, it is worth trying to find out what you can about your prospective instructors' credentials. Did they come out of a cereal box, or were they conferred by a legitimate master in an authentic martial tradition? Where did they get their permission to teach? Even among legitimate black belts, while many assist with teaching in their master's school, very few are granted license to teach independently.

What is your prospective instructor's background? Did he or she complete an apprenticeship for a reasonable period of time (a minimum of several years) in a traditional style, at a legitimate school, studying directly with an authentic master? You can pose many of these questions diplomatically during your initial interview, and sometimes by talking with other students.

Keep in mind that good schools (and bad ones) come in all sizes. Look for substance rather than outward appearance. Trust your instincts, and if at first you don't find what you're looking for, try, try again.

Good teachers are not only worth supporting; they are rare treasures. In martial arts training, aim for the best quality of instruction you can find.

The search for a good school is a quest familiar to most martial artists, and many will tell you that the school that wound up working for them just "felt right." Search diligently. When you find yours, you'll know.

The bottom line is—is this truly what you want, and do you want it badly enough to make the sacrifices necessary to achieve your goals?

If your answers to these two questions are "yes," congratulations—you are about to experience some of the most demanding—and rewarding—challenges life has to offer.

OUTFITTING YOUR OWN GYM— AFFORDABLY

Back in the section on "Setting Up," we looked at ways to create your own practice space at home, and noted that equipment and facilities can range from elaborately lavish to very simple and spare. It is the time and energy that you invest in your practice—not how fancy or plain the space and equipment are—that matters. You can, for example, easily spend $500 (or more) on mirrors for one wall alone. Hanging such a heavy collection of glass safely can involve considerable additional expense.

The "punching" or "heavy bags" used in commercial gyms start at about $75 and go up smartly from there. Sporting goods shops frequently don't stock these, and you may need to special-order them from a martial arts supply house. Factor in some hefty freight charges to get them shipped to you, especially if you get a filled bag (and, trust me, you don't want to fool around with trying to fill one). Hanging a traditional heavy bag safely and securely is no simple proposition, either.

While all other "frills" are optional, we regard these two training tools—the mirror(s) and bag(s)—as irreducible necessities. Luck-

ily, for those who are willing to invest a bit of ingenuity and elbow grease, there are more affordable solutions.

The simple "closet door" mirror shown, for example, can be found at any local hardware store for about $10.

Closet door mirror

Hot Dog Bag in Gym

There is equally good news on the heavy bag; we have developed (and patented) a simple device that works as well as (and some think even better than) the traditional heavy or "punching" bags. Parts are available at any corner hardware store, and you can build the whole thing—quickly, easily, and without any special tools—for less than $25.

This training device is a simple resistance striking target comprised of a length of chain, covered with foam rubber. (Like we said, simple.) The chain must be sufficiently heavy to offer a bit of resistance when kicked or otherwise impacted; six feet is a good length to start with. You can build the striking target to your own preference as to weight and size. Just as with traditional heavy bags, chain bags can come in different sizes and weights. We refer to bags with one chain in the center as "single-core" bags, those with two chains as "double-core" bags, and bags with three chains are "triple cores." Wrap the chain(s) in as much (or as little) foam rubber padding as you like, as explained below.

We'll walk through building a single-core target with two layers of foam covering.

In time, you may decide that you want more than one target to work with, and perhaps your second one might be a double-core target, and so on.

Needed Supplies: Start with a six-foot length of chain that looks like a good weight to you; 3/8" proof coil chain is a good starting weight. While you're at the hardware store, get a couple of lengths of pipe insulation; those foam rubber tubes are designed to be fitted over exposed water pipes to protect them from freezing in cold weather. They are usually five or six feet long, available in different diameters, and cost about two or three dollars apiece. Try to get two sizes—a smaller one (to fit your chain snugly), and a larger diameter to go over the first layer of insulating foam. Don't worry if the outside foam piece doesn't go entirely around the inner piece. What you'll end up with will probably look something like the target shown in the illustration. Although the "official" patent and trademark designations for this device are the Resistance Striking Target and the Training Chain®, they are popularly called Dragon Chains or Hot Dogs due to the elongated shape and the appearance of the two layers of insulting foam.

If you don't already have a roll of sturdy cloth tape, here's a good chance to pick one up. You'll also want a few feet—say, six or so—of rope to tie your bag at both ends, as explained below. Finally, you may want to get a "quick link" or other connecting device to help hang your bag from a ceiling hook, a rod tied to the top of a door with a couple of c-clamps, or some other handy spot.

Assembly: This is the easy part. Simply tuck the chain into the smaller-diameter foam rubber tube, as shown in the photo. The foam tubes are slit lengthwise to make this easy. Now fit the larger-diameter foam tube over the smaller one so that the slits in the tubes are on opposite sides of the chain core. Tape the foam every foot or so to keep the chain firmly secured during your sturdiest workouts. The same procedure is followed for building targets with double or triple cores. Depending on the diameter you end up with, you might want to wrap the whole thing in some sheet foam, readily available as carpet underlayment.

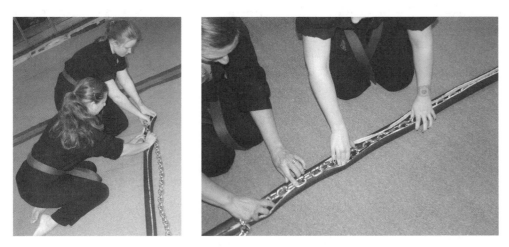

Stuffing the chain carefully into foam rubber covering.

Tie a piece of rope through the links at each end of your chain. This will help you hang the chain wherever you decide to place it, and will also enable you to tie the bottom end of the chain down to the floor, as shown in the illustration. The tie-down option is important in controlling the rebound and resistance of the chain. Depending on the situation, you can tie the bag down to a cleat or eye hook permanently fixed to the floor, or to a weight of some sort, as shown. The weight used in these illustrations is a 10-pound plate from a barbell set, but any heavy object will do.

At least a few links of chain should protrude from the top end of your device, so you can attach it with chain links, hooks, rope, or the like, to whatever you're going to be hanging it from. No links should show at the bottom of the device, however, as you may at some point be practicing foot sweeps or low kicks, and you want your foot to contact foam, not bare chain.

Et viola! You have equipped a functioning home martial arts workout space for less than $50, with enough left over for lunch. Readers wishing the convenience of ordering a "Training Chain" ready-made are invited to contact us at the addresses provided in this book (see the end of the section about Tao-Zen Ryu Shindo in the Appendices) or at our website: tao-zen.com.

Disclaimer and legal advisement on commercial usage of this device:

SAFETY NOTE: Unless you have undergone extensive "iron hand" training under an instructor genuinely qualified in this very rare specialty, have plenty of the right kind of *dit da jow* on hand, and are fully aware of the potential for damage to hand, peripheral, and even ocular nerves that can result from improper iron hand training, we do not recommend working with bare chain. The author and publisher of this book make no warranty as to the safety of resistance target training, and readers and users of such equipment assume all risk of potential loss or injury in connection therewith.

LEGAL ADVISEMENT: The Chain Resistance Striking Target invented by Master Townsend is registered with the United States Patent Office. Permission is hereby freely granted to our readers and to all private individuals to build their own "Training Chain" device for private, personal use. Any commercial use, however, must be cleared for licensing arrangements and usage permits at the addresses provided in this book.

The nomenclature "resistance striking device" and "chain target," and the names "Training Chain," "Dragon Chain," and "Hot Dog Bag" are all ™ registered with the U.S. Patent Office, and may not be used for any commercial purpose without written permission.

BIBLIOGRAPHY

Author's Note: Sometimes the best service a bibliography can provide lies in the references it does *not* include. For this list I have attempted to cull the wheat from the chaff.

TAO TE CHING, Lao Tzu
If you buy just one book in your entire life, this is the one. Many translations—I recommend Stephen Mitchell's (Harper & Row, 1988).

THE DHAMMAPADA
Many translations—highly recommended is that of Juan Mascaro (Penguin Books, 1973).

I CHING (Book of Changes)
Many translations—Richard Wilhelm's translation with Cary Baynes and a foreword by C.G. Jung is probably the definitive English version (Princeton University Press, 1950).

THE BHAGAVAD-GITA
Like the *Dhammapada,* a classic of pre-Vedic India. Many versions.

KARATE-DO: MY WAY OF LIFE, Gichin Funakoshi
The Okinawan master's autobiography details the hard life and times of a true master of karate and a real martial artist. Shotokan stylists continue his great legacy into the present day. Kodansha International (Harper & Row in the U.S.). The first English edition appeared in 1975.

KODO: Ancient Ways, Kensho Furuya
A collection of gems from the pen of Reverend Furuya, one of the foremost exponents of traditional martial arts philosophy in our age. Essential reading for every serious follower of traditional *bushido* (Ohara Publications, 1976).

THE ZEN WAY TO THE MARTIAL ARTS, Taisen Deshimaru
A refreshingly straightforward look into the philosophy underlying the "hard" Zen tradition in martial arts (E.P. Dutton, 1982).

THE WAY OF CHUANG TZU, Thomas Merton
Anything by Father Merton is always instructive, but this volume gives us
    priceless access to the gems of "Chuang Tzu" (New York: New Directions
    Publishing Corporation, 1965).

ZEN IN THE MARTIAL ARTS, Joe Hyams
A slender volume with much to say, in a very approachable way (Bantam
    Books, 1982).

TO KNOW YOURSELF, Swami Satchidananda
It would be a waste to live and miss reading this one. Straight talk from a
    straight mind. (New York: Anchor Press [Doubleday], 1978).

THE ART OF PEACE, Morihei Ueshiba
Translated by John Stevens. Cuts to the heart of true martial art. A small and
    exceedingly beautiful gem (Boston and London: Shambhala Publications,
    1992).

NEI JIA QUAN: INTERNAL MARTIAL ARTS, Jess O'Brien
 (Berkeley, California: North Atlantic Books, 2004)

ENLIGHTENMENT THROUGH AIKIDO, Kanshu Sunadomari
 (Berkeley, California: North Atlantic Books, 2004)

ON THE WARRIOR'S PATH, Danielle Bolelli
 (Berkeley, California: Frog, Ltd., 2003)

YIN-YANG IN TAIJI QUAN & DAILY LIFE, Simmone Kuo
 (Berkeley, California: North Atlantic Books, 2004)

*KRAV MAGA: HOW TO DEFEND YOURSELF AGAINST ARMED
    ASSAULT,* Imi Sde-Or
 (Berkeley, California: Frog, Ltd., 2001)

REMEMBERING THE MASTER, Sid Campbell and Greglon Lee
 (Berkeley, California: Blue Snake Books, 2006)

ACKNOWLEDGMENTS

No one ever really writes a book alone on a subject of such dynamic complexity as the martial arts. I must here offer my deepest personal thanks to some of the many others who helped make this project possible.

This book could never have happened without the inestimably generous instruction of several outstanding contemporary masters of the martial arts. Grandmaster Hak Tok Yun is recognized as "the father of Taekwondo" in Washington State. He is one of the first Korean masters to pioneer authentic training in *bushido* in America, and was one of the first to open the full syllabus of his teaching to non-Asian students. Many times over the years I suspected that he kept me on as a student primarily to test his own powers of patience. In my heart, if no longer in my ear, I still hear his corrective admonishments: "More snap! More speed! More power!" And, of course, the constant mantra of the true martial artist: "Again!" To this day, I still sometimes imagine his watchful eye upon me, keenly observing—and never missing—the minutest detail of execution of each technique.

Every performance will, ideally, be just a tad better than the last; but none has ever been exactly right—yet.

I first met Master Thomas Man-Ho King while I was working as the office manager for Grandmaster Yun's World Blackbelt Association headquarters *dojang* in Seattle. Master King came often to visit Grandmaster Yun, who was frequently away on business. Many times when this happened, Master King graciously took the time to answer my endless questions, sometimes by the hour.

As he came to realize the depth of my commitment to the martial arts, Master King began to take a kindly interest in my further education, sharing with me over ensuing years a great deal of his formidable martial expertise, experience, and wisdom. Many times he joined me and some of my students as we practiced our *bo* (long staff) under the redwoods on the shore of a nearby lake. My students probably never suspected that, long after they had departed, Master King remained, instructing me with mercilessly relentless patience in forms and techniques repeated untold numbers of times—the odd perform-ance every now and again eliciting an unim-pressed, arms-crossed "hmmph," signifying grudging acceptability. Not that any perform-ance was ever in the remotest danger of perfect execution, but occasionally a few were deemed good enough to slip by—for today.

Sensei Akio Minakami came to Seattle from Japan to teach the Okinawan martial art of Shito Ryu Karate, and in the relatively short time I was able to work as his student, he taught me far more than I suspect he ever real-ized. Much more briefly, I have had the honor to study Shen Qi Gong with one of the world's last living Taoist Qi Gong adepts, Sifu Share K. Lew.

In addition to these four outstanding mar-tial arts masters, thanks are also due to many others. Space and our readers' patience require a brief list:

To my seniors at the World Blackbelt Asso-ciation, who chose to use their experience, skills, and knowledge to encourage and assist my progress along the martial arts way; to my own students (and the families who support them), who always teach me at least as much as I teach them; and who, by their own dedication to the *budo,* help to prove and refine the syllabus of Tao-Zen Ryu Shindo and continually validate and renew the energy to carry it forward.

Thanks also are due to a very special group of martial arts colleagues, comrades on the path of *bushido:* my senior students, who per-severe to master the syllabus and remain over the years, taking time from their own fami-lies and busy lives to assume the mantle of instructor in our schools in order to pass this timeless knowledge along to others.

To the many friends who, even if they have not fully understood my intently single-minded pursuit of the martial arts, have nevertheless rolled their eyes, shaken their heads, and "hung in there" anyway, somehow forgiving all the forgone dates, missed phone calls, unpaid visits and unanswered letters, and through it all remain steadfast friends, despite the long years of unintended neglect.

While we are on the subject of neglected loved ones, a note is due to the one who is, in reality, always first on my list. Just once, nearly twenty years ago, I made a singular exception to my usual policy of not dating students. Carol and I have been happily married ever since. Despite numberless late dinners, count-less nights and weekends tending the home fires while I was off working out or teaching, testing, or helping with tournaments, and through seemingly endless "downtime" while I recovered from various injuries, this most singular exception has never failed to provide her loyal and complete (if sometimes cautious) support.

Finally, it must be noted that authors do not bring good books to the public single-handedly.

A word of appreciation is due to the folks who turn the often-disjointed jumble of raw manuscripts into coherently readable works. My thanks to Richard Grossinger and Lindy Hough at North Atlantic Books for building a publishing house with vision, heart, and global integrity, and especially to Anastasia McGhee—truly an author's dream editor. Her unique combination of broad perspective and deep insight took this project to a whole new level—a quantum jump, actually—which will make it accessible to a vastly wider range of readers than was originally intended. A master of practical diplomatic skills, she can not only herd cats but bring them in with grace and style. This book simply would not have happened—certainly not in its present form—without her.

All of these wonderful people assisted in making this book possible. If it proves helpful in time of critical need to even one person, it will have been worth the effort. Many thanks, deep respect, and great love to you all. It is rare honor indeed to travel the road of life in such august company.

—J.T.
Pioneer Hill Dojang
Winter, 2005-2006

Master J.G. Townsend

Author with Grandmaster King   Author with Grandmaster Yun

ABOUT THE AUTHOR

The Tao-Zen Ryu Shindo system of martial art was founded by Master J.G. Townsend during the waning years of the last century.

Master Townsend's formal study of several classical martial traditions—from both Eastern and Western cultures—spans more than forty years.

The principles that would one day become Tao-Zen Ryu Shindo were first tested when, as a young policeman, he patrolled the streets of a major U.S. coastal city, voluntarily working without a gun.

In the early 1990s, he received black belts in each of the two largest worldwide systems of Taekwondo, and additionally, the very rarely granted honor of independent teaching permission, in direct transmission from two of the world's highest-ranking Taekwondo authorities—Grandmaster Hak Tok Yun (10th Dan, World Taekwondo Federation, WTF) and Grandmaster Thomas Man-Ho King (9th Dan, International Taekwondo Federation [ITF] and WTF). Ten years after the establishment of the Tao-Zen Ryu system, he was further honored with the conferral of his present title, *Sabum Nim* (Master).

On November 17, 2001, in a ceremony at a major northwestern U.S. regional martial arts tournament, Grandmaster Hak Tok Yun formally designated eight of his senior students, including Master Townsend, as his direct successors in the arts—the highest honor a martial arts master can bestow.

Some call Tao-Zen Ryu
a Western art,
because it first sprouted here.

Some consider it an
Eastern art,
because its roots are
so deeply Oriental.
I say let it be for the world.
Remember that we are
only pruning
the greenest branches
of a tree with ancient roots.

—Master Townsend
Pioneer Hill Dojang
Summer 2001